CHRIST IN BANGLADESH

CHRIST IN BANGLADESH

James and Marti Hefley

HARPER & ROW, PUBLISHERS

New York, Evanston, San Francisco, London

FIRST EDITION

STANDARD BOOK NUMBER: 06-063801-X

LIBRARY OF CONGRESS CATALOG CARD NUMBER: 72-79956

Dedicated to
the Christian missionaries of Bangladesh,
who in the crucible of suffering
became Bengalis themselves

Contents

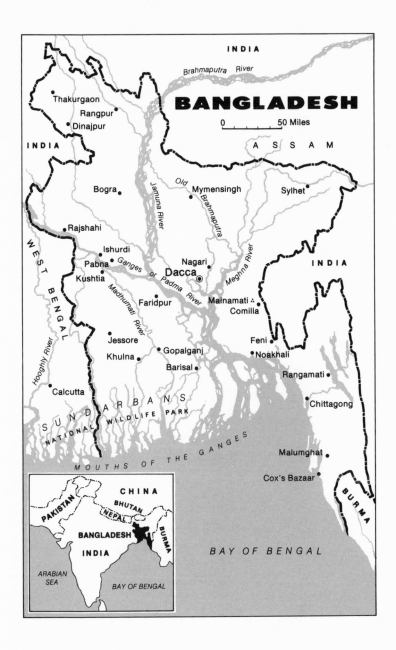

CHRIST IN BANGLADESH

I

Storm of the Century

A TIROS WEATHER SATELLITE first saw the ugly ring-shaped storm, spinning counterclockwise around its evil eye, moving up the cyclonic Bay of Bengal toward the fan-shaped delta of East Pakistan.

The cyclone was still far offshore when the satellite's photo report reached the provincial capital of Dacca, two hundred miles inland, on the afternoon of November 11, 1970. *"Moha bipod shonket* (big danger coming)" was broadcast, but a clerk forgot to include a code number indicating the 160-mph force of the oncoming storm. Few of the three million Bengalis living in the marshy delta took the warning seriously.

But at Barisal, the most Christianized town in the largely Muslim region, Anglican, Baptist, and Catholic missionaries battened down for a strong blow. By 10:30 P.M. the winds were already shrieking past at 50 mph.

Under cover of darkness and weather three thieves crept up to the Anglican mission, overpowered the night watchman, and invaded the compound. They took money and personal effects from the British sisters in the first house; then, with one standing guard, two forced Sister Joan to lead them into the quarters of sixty-six year-old Father McBeth.

Sister Joan's cry was too late. The tough old pastor, who had been in East Pakistan since 1933, lunged for the robbers and in the struggle was knifed in the heart. He collapsed in a pool of blood and Sister Joan fainted away.

The incident was a symbol of greater tragedy to follow.

The robbers escaped under cover of the winds that kept increasing in force. Further inland the people of East Pakistan felt no alarm at the high winds and rain. They slept peacefully and awakened to the Muslim holy day on Friday. Stores and offices were closed and prayers to Allah droned from community mosques. Neighbor talk was mainly about the upcoming democratic elections, the first in twenty-three years. Could Sheik Mujib's Awami League party win a majority in the new Assembly? If so, millions of Bengalis devoutly believed the much-imprisoned Mujib would set things right and break the stranglehold of the domineering West Pakistanis.

Exactly at noon a Thai International jet touched down at the Dacca airport. Jim and Betty McKinley, Southern Baptist missionaries, were returning with their three children from a Malaysian vacation. As they pushed through customs, thirteen-year-old dimpled Cherry remarked that the date was Friday the thirteenth. "Do you believe we'll have bad luck getting home?" she asked her Kentuckian father. Jim grinned and drawled that he didn't think so.

A creaky taxi carried them to their mission's guest house on Road Four, a few blocks from the home of controversial Sheik Mujib. Here they picked up their jeep and drove southeast toward their station at Feni. They saw broken branches along the road but this was not unusual in windy November. Arriving home at six, they saw the hibiscus hedge blown over, and knew there had been a storm. Still they felt no alarm. Twelve years in East Pakistan had accustomed them to frequent heavy blows from the Bay of Bengal, only twenty-one miles away.

They all stayed busy around the house the next day. Betty and the girls seldom went out in the Muslim community where women were expected to stay in seclusion. That evening Jim tuned to the Voice of America and heard that a powerful cyclone had smashed the delta. The damage and death toll was yet unknown. He now suspected for the first time that something bad must have happened.

Sunday morning the McKinleys met for worship with the one other Christian family in Feni. Afterwards they heard Radio Pakistan from Dacca saying there had been a storm, but that foreign reports of a major disaster were exaggerated.

Monday morning, R. T. Buckley, another Southern Baptist missionary, arrived. McKinley suggested that the two men drive toward the ocean and try to find out the truth. Just before reaching the levee they met a pale Pakistani official.

"Bodies, bodies everywhere!" he moaned. "In the trees. On the beach. Floating in the ocean. It's horrible!"

They drove on and soon began seeing bloated bodies grotesquely entwined in debris, so many they stopped counting. Here and there they found survivors, numb and dazed, some with chests lacerated from climbing trees, wailing "Allah wills! Allah wills!"

McKinley and Buckley introduced themselves as "Bible people," the name Jim was known by for operating a Bible reading room in Feni.

"What happened?" they asked.

From the gasped replies, the missionaries deduced that the driving winds had pushed a giant tidal wave up the river channels. The water had then come crashing back across the marshy rice and jute fields destroying almost everything in its path.

The missionaries had brought no tools or relief supplies. Faces drawn and eyes reddened from the sight of the horror, they promised to return and help the survivors.

Monday, the provincial governor, a West Pakistani, down-played the tragedy on the radio, saying "only" sixteen thousand were dead.

But by this time the world knew that something catastrophic had indeed taken place in the densely populated region. The foreign press was calling it the storm of the century.

Forty countries, including communist China, pledged aid through the Red Cross. Caritas International, coordinating relief agency of the Catholic church, sent $100,000. CARE and The Catholic Medical Mission Board in New York dispatched medicines, antityphoid vaccine, vitamins, and water purification tablets. Medical Assistance Programs of Wheaton, Illinois, airshipped three and a half tons of medicines. Church World Service, the evangelical World Relief Commission, and three Baptist groups sent funds to missionaries.

Foreign relief helicopters swarmed over the hard-hit offshore islands, dropping food. The odor from decaying bodies was so intense that some pilots became nauseated. An American chopper carrying U.S. Ambassador Joseph S. Farland and food landed and was almost torn apart by starving Bengalis.

It was all quite embarrassing to the Pakistani government, which in the far west had been callous from the start. The Pak navy had not been ordered to search for survivors, though three days after the cyclone people had been seen floating, still alive. Pak army helicopters had sat on their pads, leaving tons of stored food in warehouses. Soldiers from the western wing who were stationed in the east lounged in their barracks, disdaining to help bury the dead. Provincial officials huffily refused Indian planes, loaded with relief supplies, permission to land at nearby Chittagong because the crews did not have visas. Finally, thirteen days after Black Thursday, President Yahya Khan flew from the west and visited the area. By this time the world press was calling it the greatest natural disaster of the twentieth century.

Aware of the disaster and funded by their supporting churches in the United States and Europe, Christian missionaries moved in to help.

Jim McKinley and three Southern Baptist colleagues saw that purification tablets were only a stopgap solution to the water problem. So they obtained funds from their Board to sink two-hundred tube wells for uncontaminated water.

The need was so desperate, they worked man-killing hours under the broiling sun. Each day began at 3:30 when they rose for breakfast, then loaded the long inch-and-a-half-diameter pipes into a truck and drove from the McKinleys' house to the stricken area. Starting a well was a simple affair of pushing a section of pipe about eighteen inches into the spongy ground, filling it with water, wiggling bamboo beside it, and working the pipe up and down. By adding water and sections of pipe as the tube worked down and drawing the sand up by suction, a hundred-foot-deep well could be sunk in one day, a filter installed, and the hole topped off with a pitcher pump. One well could mean the difference between disease-contaminated water and pure water for a whole village.

The Baptists and their hired helpers moved from site to site, gingerly walking around mounds of dirt that frequently covered bodies only partially buried. At most sites they could hear parents wailing for lost children. One man told them he had lost twenty-five of twenty-nine members of his greater family.

"We can't control our tears when we sit down to eat," McKinley wrote his mission headquarters in Virginia. "God has been so good to us, and yet so near are these hundreds of thousands whose lives are so unbearable."

Calvin Olson, a lean sandy-haired native of Minnesota, led a team for his Assembly of God mission across stricken Patar Char Island where forty percent of the people had died and every home was destroyed. They built seventeen-by-nine-foot houses, costing $100 each, walled with woven bamboo and roofed with corrugated tin. Some of the grateful recipients told of clinging to treetops and being washed twenty miles away.

All of the missionaries who worked among the survivors heard heart-stopping tales of the terrible night. A woman told Adventist Jabil Jacobs, a Tennessean of Lebanese descent, of having her baby swept from her arms as she clung to a palm tree in the rushing water. A few minutes later another baby was swept into her arms—alive. "Allah took one child and gave me another," she said while hugging the child to her bosom. The Adventists helped 1,100 families with food, cooking utensils, and medicines. Of the 1,100 only six reported no loss of an immediate family member.

Lanky Phil Parshall, of the International Christian Fellowship, heard of a teen-age girl who stayed afloat by holding the tail of a cow all night. The next day she joined a boy clinging to a floating table. Two days later a ship pulled them aboard.

Surveying the hundreds of mounds under trees denuded of leaves, Parshall wrote, "Explain it? No, the clichés leave me cold. My understanding is stunned. I can only say that even after that dread night God is still God and in Him is my trust."

The known death toll on the isolated offshore islands was past two-hundred thousand and still rising when Pope Paul stopped briefly in Dacca on his way to Manila.

Notre Dame-educated Archbishop Theotonius Ganguly met him at the airport and reported on the tragedy. Christians were doing all they could, the Bengali prelate said; Catholics numbered barely 100,000 in a population of 75 million and Protestants were even fewer. The pope grimaced at the tales of horror and urged all Christians in the stricken province to "hope in a better tomorrow."

As the pope spoke Catholic missionaries were hard at work with their Protestant counterparts. They were all so few in the populous province that many were on a first-name basis. They had studied the difficult Bengali language, an offshoot of ancient Sanskrit, together in the school at Barisal operated by the Catholics. On overland trips they lodged and ate at one another's stations. Protestant missionary mothers had their babies at the Catholic Holy Family Hospital in Dacca. The Protestant International church for English-speaking foreigners met at Holy Cross College in Dacca. Southern Baptist Troy Bennett, who played tennis regularly with a priest friend, put it succinctly: "In a country where all Christians make up less than one half of one percent of the population you have to get to know one another. We may differ in theology and church practices, but we are close as friends and colleagues in helping people."

In the first days after the cyclone the minority Hindus revived from the shock and pitched in to help patch up their losses. The fatalistic Muslims were inclined to "sit back" as Father Richard Timm noted, "and wait for Allah to hit them again."

Father Timm, a tall, broad-shouldered, bearded, scientist-theologian with long, flowing, dark hair, was then president of Notre Dame College in Dacca. He shepherded a squad of thirty-five students who distributed tents and other relief supplies. He and other Catholic missionaries suggested that their individual efforts needed coordination. The provincial Catholic hierarchy responded by setting up the province-wide Christian Organization for Relief and Rehabilitation (CORR). CORR would be the funnel for funds and relief goods from all Catholic agencies domestic and foreign.

Catholics and Protestants divided up the territory, with CORR concentrating on the eastern Noakhali side of the delta and adjacent islands and Protestants tackling the ravaged areas south of Barisal. There was plenty of work for all.

For example, a CORR survey of tiny, fifty-eight-square-mile Char Jabbar Island showed 4,744 persons dead and 14,-133 surviving, ninety-eight percent of the houses destroyed or heavily damaged, ninety percent of the rice crop damaged, plus roads and levees washed out. Destitute farmers were paid to repair roads and levees. Twenty-one power tillers, 770 bullocks, 600 plows, 235 tons of rice seeds, 92 barrels of insecticides, and other necessities were purchased and brought by boat to the islands. Prefab houses, costing $170 each, were shipped from factories in nearby Chittagong. Wells were sunk, home tanks cleaned, and thousands of washing and cooking utensils provided. CORR's aim was not temporary relief, but total rehabilitation covering the entire spectrum of life.

By February it seemed apparent that upwards of half a million people had indeed died. Yet the rehabilitation was proceeding smoothly. Farmers were planting crops; fishermen reaping good hauls of fish. Levees were rising and roads and bridges being restored. The spirits of the people were springing back like bent bamboo.

But the Christian missionaries were less than optimistic. They sensed that the winds of political instability were rising fast.

II

Betrayal of the Bengalis

THE RACKING INDO-PAKISTANI political and religious conflicts of the past quarter century have puzzled Americans and Europeans, who wonder why they can't get along. Perhaps the convolutions will be less enigmatic if we transpose their history to the American side of the globe.

Imagine the United States peopled with four hundred million impoverished Hindus and Muslims and ruled by the British until 1947, the Muslims fervently holding to the unity of one God, Allah; the Hindus worshiping a pantheon of deities. Their constant conflicts would have nationalistic overtones.

A survey would show most Muslims inhabiting watery "Florida" and the western deserts and mountains of "California, Nevada, and Arizona." Most Hindus would live between. The British solution would be to dismember their possession into three sections and grant independence to two nations. "Florida" and the western region where Muslims were in the majority would become Pakistan. The larger middle section where Hindus predominated would remain India.

This partition would lead to religious riots, mass killings, and migrating waves of people as politicians jockeyed for power and battles raged over boundaries. An apostle of non-violence (Mahatma Gandhi) would try to stop the blood-letting by nonviolent protest and be assassinated by a Hindu fanatic. By 1965 only the U.N. could prevent bloody border fighting from mushrooming into full-scale war. After the cease-fire the two countries would continue to eye each other angrily at dagger's length.

Apart from its traditional enemy, Pakistan had critical divisions besides geography.

Not all easterners shared the Islamic faith; Hindus made up fifteen percent of the east's population.

Westerners were tall, long-nosed, light, wheat-and–meat-eaters and spoke mainly the Urdu and Sindhi languages. They were more like the energetic peoples who are strewn across the arc of Islamic land that stretches as far as Turkey.

Easterners were short, dark-skinned, slim-waisted rice-and–fish-eaters and more like the masses of South and Southeast Asia. They spoke the flowing poetic, Sanskrit–related language of their Bengali fathers.

Even the dress was different. The ruling Punjabi elite of the west inclined toward European-style clothing. The Bengalis, Muslim and Hindu, fancied the traditional dress of India: the women in graceful, wrap-around saris and the men in shirt and *lunghi* skirt.

The west dominated the east, attempting to force the Urdu language upon the Bengalis, siphoning precious foreign exchange from the fertile east, and taking the lion's share of billions in foreign aid. The Bengalis—sixty percent of the total population living on fifteen percent of the land area—grew more resentful toward western governmental, economic, and military domination with each passing year. They were held in the confederation only by a military government that policed the east with soldiers and appointed many key civil officials from the west.

Agitation and strikes finally forced President Yahya Khan to announce the first democratic parliamentary elections. He gambled that the argumentative Bengalis would scatter their votes among political parties, preventing the troublesome Sheik Mujib Rahman's Awami League party from getting a majority. The much-imprisoned Mujib wanted eastern control of its own provincial affairs, leaving only defense and foreign relations to the central government in the west.

But Yahya Khan's strategy was spoiled by the insensibility of his own government toward the Bengali survivors of the terrible cyclone. The callous disregard of Bengali suffering proved to be the ultimate slap in the face. Three weeks after the storm, the subjugated Bengalis voted Mujib's party a clear majority (167 of 313 representatives). Mujib himself—tall for a Bengali and grandfatherly, with hair turning gray—became the symbol of liberty. Everywhere he appeared in his familiar loose black vest drooping over billowing white cotton pajama pants the crowds shouted *"Joi Bangla!* (Victory to Bengal)."

President Khan saw that Mujib would certainly be named head of state by his majority of representatives. He postponed the National Assembly to March 3, 1971, and began bargaining with Mujib for concessions. As they talked, the fuse of Bengali patience burned short. Strikes and demonstrations kept the country in continual upheaval.

Such was the political scenario developing around the Christian missionaries and Bengali nationals at the turn of the new year.

The tense political situation did not prevent the Assemblies of God from going ahead with a Billy Graham-style evangelistic crusade.

Clifford Burgess, the evangelist, was an instant attraction. Curious Bengalis asked him if he was a CIA agent. "No," he replied smiling. "I am an agent of Jesus Christ. I came to tell you about Him."

"You must be very rich to come so far," an awed young man declared.

"No. There are friends in America who care about you. They sent me and the missionaries who have been helping people hurt by the storm."

This brought nods all around and murmurs of "America is our friend." The next five nights of preaching resulted in over a hundred professions of faith, an unusually high response from Muslims and Hindus.

Meanwhile, Sheik Mujib was unbending in discussions with the military ruler. Yahya Khan tried a new tack—toughness. He postponed the assembly again—to an unspecified time— declared martial law with the army in control, and replaced the civilian governor in Dacca with General "Tikka" (meaning "Red Hot") Khan, a tall Punjabi not noted for mercy.

The Bengalis answered tit for tat. A crippling province-wide strike brought most business to a halt. Angry mobs roamed city streets, looting shops owned by non-Bengalis. Mujib called for *satyagraha* (nonviolent civil disobedience) until the people were given their rights.

West Pakistani businessmen, industrialists, and professional men saw the handwriting on the wall and raced for the Dacca airport. A few anxious foreigners joined them. Passenger jets came winging in from the west, loaded with hard-eyed soldiers dressed as civilians. The soldiers disembarked at Dacca to beef up the regular army and the evacuees took their seats for the return trip.

The Reverend Bob Burns, publications secretary for the Association of Baptists for World Evangelism, drove into Dacca in early March from a filming trip at his mission's hospital in the far south near the Burma border. Baptist deacon Mark Tucker, director of maintenance at the U.S. AID-funded Cholera Research Hospital, sped him to the airport in an ambulance. They found the unlighted terminal jammed with West Pakistanis pushing and shoving to reach the exit gate. The latrines had overflowed and the air stank.

"There are no planes today," an army officer told them. "Maybe tomorrow." Seeing Burns's address on his luggage, the officer smiled, "You Americans are our friends. The Indians will start a war, but our soldiers are very brave and will win. You will help us."

Tucker took Burns back in the ambulance the next two days in succession until the mission photographer got a departure pass. Tucker, a beefy, balding Texan with a gravel voice, shrugged when Burns asked if he would be leaving soon. "I sent my wife out a few days ago," he replied. "I'll stay and hold the fort with the missionaries."

After standing in line all day, Burns was permitted into the departure lounge. The customs formalities were handled by three uniformed men. "You have bomb?" the first asked. Burns shook his head and was passed on. The second asked, "You have gun?" and the third, "You have knife?" When Burns showed a penknife in response to the last question, the Pakistani scowled, "You don't have knife! Go on." Late that afternoon his DC–8 jet, with evacuees sitting in the center aisle, lumbered off the ground.

The rising unrest forced President Khan to call the Assembly for March 25. Sheik Mujib declared before a half million cheering Bengalis crowded on the Dacca race course that he would not attend unless martial law was canceled, soldiers sent back to their barracks, and shootings investigated. Meanwhile, he said, Bengalis would not pay taxes and would continue *satyagraha.*

By mid-March East Pakistan was in a frenzy. Red and green Bengali flags rose faster than western soldiers could take them down. Mass prison breaks, riots, and brick throwing churned the cities into turmoil. Armed soldiers patrolled some streets; Awami Leaguers armed only with bamboo sticks and flags marched along others.

The evangelical churches in Dacca canceled a missionary convention at the last minute, then went ahead after three guest speakers arrived from abroad. While evacuation planes roared overhead, they heard Dr. Christy Wilson from Kabul, Afghanistan, speak on James 1:2: "Count it all joy, my brethren, when you meet various trials."

A week later President Khan flew in and asked for more discussions. While these talks were going on a Bengali mob surrounded West Pakistani troops unloading ammunition ships in Chittagong. The troops opened fire, killing thirty-five. Sheik Mujib angrily issued a fresh strike call for March 27.

Khan kept up a façade of negotiations, then suddenly flew home without notice on the evening of the twenty-fifth. His late evening jet had hardly cleared the runway when the fresh troops flown in on the evacuation planes slipped quietly from their barracks. They joined soldiers on patrol to "teach the Bengalis a lesson."

Leslie Wenger, the tall, white-haired, senior British Baptist missionary in Dacca, was awakened by a loud bang. The British Baptists were the oldest Protestant group in East Pakistan, dating their mission to Bible translator William Carey who sailed into the Bay of Bengal in 1795. Born in Barisal in

1908 of missionary parents, Wenger and his wife, Freda, had
seen their share of disturbances. He frequently commented
that the narrow streets around their compound in old Dacca
were quiet only from 3:00 to 3:05 A.M.

The quiet did not come that night. The Wengers ran to
their windows and saw Punjabi soldiers racing under the
shadows of buildings, hurling fire bombs against shuttered
bamboo shops. They watched the flimsy buildings catch fire,
crackle in the humid night, and light up the sky. They heard
screams and saw frightened people pouring into the street
behind the soldiers.

Two miles west, near the University of Dacca, Phil Parshall
was sleeping soundly, tired from preparing Bible correspon-
dence lessons. About 2 A.M. the clink, clink of bricks being
thrown into the middle of Satmashjid Road broke his sleep.
Parshall awakened his wife, Julie, and two other couples, the
Bill Barnetts and the Ed Welches. They climbed to the roof
of the ICF mission house and watched Bengali neighbors
make primitive roadblocks. Within half an hour the soldiers
arrived and the warm night was filled with gunfire, shouts,
and screams. They saw the first building go up in flames, then
another and another, until the skyline around them was
ringed with fire. In the light of the fires Bengalis were hurling
bricks and sticks at Punjabi soldiers firing semiautomatic
rifles. As Parshall later recounted, "The purgatory of Bengal
suddenly matured into a raging, swirling whirlpool of Hell."

About 3 A.M. a military convoy stopped outside the mission
gate. Peering over the roof's edge, Parshall saw eight com-
bat-dressed soldiers pointing rifles at him. Unable to understand their Urdu commands, he quickly retreated from view.

The sound of the flimsy roadblocks being thrown up also
awakened the Calvin Olsons who lived above the Assembly
of God Bengali church a half mile from the modernistic In-

tercontinental Hotel. Moments later they heard the pop-pop-pop of automatic gunfire, then the rumble of tanks and armored vehicles moving along New Eskaton Road, the broad street behind their house. They raced for an inner bathroom just as a bullet burst a window and slammed into a bookcase behind them.

West of the Dacca airport, the Adventist compound was in an ethnically mixed area. Bamboo Bengali huts adjoined the better homes of Biharis. The Biharis, only two percent of the population, were Muslims who had left India after the partition to become the trustful managers for the West Pakistani elite. They spoke the "official" Urdu language and held the best jobs. Foreigners could tell them from Bengalis only by language and their superior positions in society. The Bengalis, who toiled in the fields and factories, knew them on sight and regarded them as bootlicking aliens.

Late on the night of the twenty-fifth a Bihari neighbor climbed over the wall of the Adventist compound with chilling news. "My brother-in-law, the district commissioner, just phoned me. He said the end of the Bengalis has come."

Jabil and Lois Jacobs climbed to the roof of their house and saw tongues of flame leaping up across the city. As they watched in growing apprehension, cries came from below. Their Bengali employees were frightened.

They hurried down and invited the employees who worked in the adjoining school and printing plant into their living room. "We're not sure what's happening," the slim, brown-eyed Jacobs said softly, "but we are sure the Lord is with us." He thumbed to Psalm 91:1–2 in his worn Bible and read, "He that dwelleth in the secret place of the most High shall abide under the shadow of the Almighty. I will say of the Lord, He is my refuge and my fortress: my God; in Him will I trust."

The burning and shooting continued through the night. Near sunrise the Jacobses were startled by twenty-five to thirty armed soldiers—Bengalis—coming over the wall. Jacobs saw that they belonged to the East Pakistan Rifles (National Guard) and were scared. "Please let us stay with you, Holy Man," they begged. "The Punjabis are killing all Bengalis in uniform."

Jacobs permitted them to hide.

A few minutes later Jacobs heard the sound of a moving crowd. He stood on a box and looked over the six-foot brick wall that faced the road. Streams of Bengali refugees were coming out of Dacca. The stronger were pulling carts or pedaling rickshaws piled with personal belongings. Old men, mothers with babes in arms, and small children trotted to keep up.

"Where are you bound?" Jacobs asked from behind the wall.

A cart pusher who never stopped grunted, "India. There is no hope here."

Jacobs called his wife. While they were watching the exodus, the Bengali soldiers they had sheltered emerged in T-shirts and *lunghis.* Jacobs helped them over the wall to join the flight. "Pray for us, Holy Man," the last one said. "We don't know if we'll live to see you again."

All day the Bengali refugees streamed by going east. The next morning they heard the roar of a different crowd. From their roof they watched a Bihari mob looting and burning the homes of the Bengalis who had fled. Though this crowd appeared out of control, the missionaries went ahead with Saturday services for their employees.

At 3 P.M. fellow Adventists Dr. and Mrs. James Van Blaricum and their son drove into the compound. They had been two days coming from Gopalganj, only sixty miles to the southeast. Enroute they had been sprayed with bullets by Pak soldiers, but the only casualty was their son, Charlie, who had a nicked ear. Somehow they had driven through the Bihari mob safely and reached the compound.

The Biharis rampaged through the night and into Sunday. They set houses afire within fifty feet of the west wall and within two hundred feet of the eastern side of the compound. The missionaries were sweating from the waves of heat when a reassuring voice called, "Don't be afraid. You are in a sacred place."

The "lesson" in repression that the Pak military taught was from the script of the ancient Mongols. Seven centuries before, under the command of another Khan (Genghis Khan), the Mongols had murdered and plundered their way to a vast Eurasian empire.

But the Bengalis refused to heed the lesson. Sheik Mujib proclaimed Bangladesh (Bengal nation) to be free and independent before he was arrested and spirited away from his Dacca home. Rebels, calling themselves Mukti Bahini (Freedom Brothers), seized the radio station in the second city, Chittagong, and broadcast Mujib's proclamation with instructions for "resistance at all costs."

The "bamboo telegraph" spread the news up and down the odd-shaped land of Bengal, from Thakurgaon in the north to the resort town of Cox's Bazaar along the white sand beaches in the south. The missionaries still helping the cyclone survivors in the offshore islands were the last to hear.

Friday, the twenty-sixth, bearded Father Timm, the strapping priest adviser for CORR on Manpura Island, boarded a steamer. He was off to purchase cattle for farmers whose plow animals had drowned in the tidal bore. He got off at a landing and walked two hours to the town of Bhola where he hoped to find animals for sale. Arriving about 8 P.M., he was immediately rushed by a hostile crowd screaming, "Punjabi! Punjabi! Enemy!"

The tall, deeply tanned educator was wearing surplus U.S. army fatigues. Throwing up large hands, he shouted, "Not Punjabi. American Christian missionary."

But the crowd pressed in on him until he could see the hatred burning in dark eyes.

"Wait!" a commanding voice called at the last instant. An Awami League political leader pushed through the crowd and quizzed the missionary. Satisfied he was not a Punjabi, the politician escorted Father Timm to a second floor balcony where he could be heard by all.

Father Timm could speak fluent Bengali. Looking down into the sea of intense dark faces, he gave a rousing address, relating how he had devoted his life to educating their sons and was now trying to help the poor cyclone victims.

Father Timm's troubles were not over. His returning boat was caught in a storm and driven north toward the mainland. When his friends at the relief site on Manpura Island did not hear from him for three days, they sent word to Dacca that he was dead. On the fourth day, he appeared—alive, though haggard and weak.

Back in Dacca, Tikka Khan was having problems with foreign correspondents whom he had tried to bottle up in hotels. He finally ordered them expelled and their notes and film confiscated. But they knew enough to tell the world that up to three hundred thousand civilians had been slaughtered. The military governor howled that Pakistan had been slandered. He conceded there had been some killing by rebel agitators, but said the military now had everything under control.

The missionaries in Dacca knew better.

The three American families at the International Christian

Fellowship house heard that a massacre had taken place at the nearby University of Dacca. When the army lifted the curfew for six hours on the twenty-eighth, Phil Parshall, Bill Barnett, and Ed Welch drove through deserted streets to the campus.

A small band of angry students stopped their car and led them first to a mass grave where blood still oozed from the ground, then to a servants' compound. "Look in each room," a young Bengali requested. "See what the brave Punjabis did."

In the first room they saw a mother crumpled in a corner, her lifeless arms entwining two dead children. The second room was empty but bloodstained. The third contained an obviously pregnant woman dead and covered with flies. The fourth was a replay of the first: two children in the arms of their mother. Nauseated and shocked, they headed for an exit.

The following day the three men drove to the Dacca boat terminal, the nerve system of a country laced with waterways. The terminal was ghostlike and deserted. But the splotches of human blood that stained the walls and floor told the story. Outside, they were told that the army had shot everyone in sight, even the beggars.

There were only 160 Protestant missionaries in East Pakistan at the time and about an equal number of Catholics from abroad. Most were Americans. The American consulate in Dacca advised the American Protestant mothers and children and other nonessential adults, both Protestant and Catholic, to leave on evacuation planes. If they stayed, their safety could not be guaranteed.

But few were willing to go. The Muslim military government had always been tough on visas for foreign church workers. They feared reentry permits would be denied.

Most other Americans were not so reluctant and headed for the airport. One who stayed was Mark Tucker. He was at the International Church the following Sunday to hear Phil Parshall sum up the feelings of the foreign Christian community. Parshall compared Dacca to the prophet Jeremiah's ravished Jerusalem as he read from the first chapter of Lamentations: "How doth the city sit solitary, that was full of people! How is she become a widow! She that was great among the nations. . . . She weepeth sore in the night, and her tears are on her cheeks: among all her lovers she hath none to comfort her. . . ."(1–2).

Then, speaking more to the world than to his small audience, he asked the question of verse 12: "Is it nothing to you all ye that pass by?"

III

Profiles in Courage

BY MONDAY, following the brutal Thursday evening massacres, Dacca was like a city of the dead. The rickshaw bells and blaring taxi horns were silent. Most of the population of the old capital that dated to the reign of the Great Mughals in 1608 had fled to their ancestral villages or across the border of India that horseshoed the province on three sides. Those remaining cowered inside their homes, emerging only to buy food during brief liftings of the curfew.

The mission houses were full of fearful Bengali Hindus and Christians who babbled their tales of horror.

Cal and Marian Olson were hosts and protectors at the Assemblies of God place, which contained an auditorium, bookroom, and missionary apartment on the second floor.

Hindus, they were told, had been special targets. Soldiers would snatch away a man's *lunghi*. If revealed to be uncircumcised, they shot him on the assumption he was Hindu, shouting, "Death to the *maloun* (cursed one)! Victory to Allah!" Girls had been raped and killed in front of parents, or carried off screaming.

The Olsons had been East Pakistan residents since 1954 and knew the Bengali penchant for exaggeration. But the terror in the eyes of their Bengali guests bespoke truth. Cal decided to venture out in his white Volkswagen and see for himself.

With a Bengali Christian he drove across Dacca. Entering the Hindu quarter, they smelled the bodies before they saw them. They lay grotesquely along gutters and doorsteps and inside fire blackened houses: venerable patriarchs with beards stiffened by blood; mothers with babies hanging in the crook of arms stiff in rigor mortis; children whose sightless eyes seemed fixed on crows circling overhead. They saw no guns near any victims. It was cold, vicious murder and the two men, oriental and occidental, walked among the dead and wept their tear ducts dry.

Back in the apartment Cal told his wife their findings, sparing her the grisly details. "I agree with you that we should stay," she said. "If ever our Bengali friends needed us, they need us now."

Two hundred and fifty miles south the ill-organized, ragtag Mukti Bahini were still resisting in Chittagong, though armed only with a few stolen rifles and bows and arrows. But the better equipped and wily Pak army was steadily whittling them down. In one ploy the Paks forced Bengalis to ride on the front of a truck shouting, *"Joi Bangla!"* When Muktis emerged from hiding spots with answering cries, soldiers hidden in the back riddled them with machine gun fire.

A bitter battle raged around the Baptist chapel and bookroom operated by the Association of Baptists for World Evangelism. Forty strong, the Abweys, as fellow missionaries called them, were the largest non-Catholic foreign group in the province. Members of an independent agency supported by several Baptist groups in the U.S., the A.B.W.E. missionaries were not connected ecclesiastically with the four other Baptist groups (U.S. Southern, British, Australian and New Zealand) working in the larger area to the north. The Abwey ministry was concentrated 65 miles south at the Malumghat Hospital which had the reputation of being the best medical facility in the province.

The U.S. consulate in Dacca recommended that the three Abwey missionaries in Chittagong, bachelor minister Reid Minich and publication workers Ernajean Lockerbie and Lynn Silvernail, evacuate. But the two young women were sheltering six Bengali teen-age girls and other Bengalis from marauding Pak soldiers. Minich wanted to keep an eye on mission property and help his Bengali brothers in their trial and danger.

They decided to take their charges to the hospital and confer with their colleagues about future plans. Tying American flags to two jeeps, they set out along the narrow, pot-holed road that was an obstacle course to anyone traveling south.

Ten years before, Dr. Viggo ("Vic") Olsen, a white-haired Gregory Peck, and colleagues had established the hospital in "the neediest place in the world." Describing East Pakistan as "something like a lopsided amoeba with a foot sticking down into Burma," he noted that the "foot" was an unevangelized gap between territory covered by two great pioneer Baptist missionaries of South Asia, William Carey and Adoniram Judson. Surveys showed that the area was populated by Bengali Muslims, Hindus and Buddhists, plus loin-clothed hill tribesmen who spoke exotic unwritten languages. Christians were almost as rare as ice storms. There seemed to be every disease in the medical books and some that weren't.

The hospital charged only fourteen cents a day for a ward bed, but had four private rooms for more well-to-do patients who sometimes were flown or driven from the far north for treatment. Dr. Olsen and his bearded associate, Dr. Donn Ketcham, were renowned for their skills in an area where life expectancy still hung at thirty-two years.

The doctors, nurses, and other hospital personnel were glad to see their co-missioners from Chittagong. There had been no fighting around the hospital, but wild rumors had been flying.

Reid Minich related the happenings in Chittagong and conveyed the recommendation from the consulate. They met in the Ketcham home so they wouldn't alarm the national staff and discussed what action to take.

"I can't see that we all should leave," Vic Olsen said as he took a cup of coffee from Kitty Ketcham. "We're technically neutrals—here to serve everyone in the name of Christ. But leaving or staying should be something for each individual or couple to decide for themselves."

A family with small children and three ladies felt for valid reasons they should fly to West Pakistan. There they could comfort Abwey teenagers in high school at a mission school. Reid Minich volunteered to drive them to Chittagong and see them on a plane. He would remain in the city to look after mission property and help sustain Bengali Christians and other friends. Ernajean and Lynn would remain at the hospital for the time being.

Minich left with his passengers on Monday, April 5. The next day the "bamboo telegraph" reported fighting between Mukti Bahinis and Pak soldiers between the hospital and Chittagong. The missionaries at Malumghat hoped their colleagues had reached the city safely.

Wednesday, after a long schedule of surgery, Vic Olsen, Donn Ketcham and colleague Jay Walsh were confronted by a delegation of Mukti rebels demanding guns and ammunition. The three Americans looked solemnly at the intense young men. "No," Dr. Olsen said. "You'll use our hunting guns to kill people. It isn't right for us to be involved. We're here to save lives, not take them."

The rebels seemed to understand and left. But the missionaries felt they should take turns standing guard.

Two nights later physiotherapist Larry Golin was on duty at the hospital when two jeeploads of Muktis roared down the road that led to the missionary residences about a half mile back. He jumped into his car and overtook them. They refused to tell him what they wanted, and insisted on seeing Dr. Olsen and the others. Jay Walsh, the current chairman of the Abwey mission, the two doctors, and missionary Mel Beals came out rubbing their eyes. "The army has bombed our radio station at Chittagong," the rebel spokesman said. "We want to place the radio here and broadcast from the hospital grounds."

The request caught the missionaries by surprise. They wondered how the request could be denied and the hospital be preserved. "We're a democratic group and can't make that decision without a meeting and further discussion," Vic Olsen said. "Come back tomorrow after we've talked about it."

The Muktis returned ahead of schedule while the missionaries were still meeting. Vic Olsen's colleagues prayed while he went to talk with them. He wondered what he could possibly say to change their minds.

By the time he reached the end of the driveway an answer he believed came from God was in his mind. "Let's think about a couple of things," he suggested calmly. "If you put the station here, the planes will bomb it and the hospital. The battle of Chittagong isn't going well. The soldiers will soon be coming this way. They may shoot you, your wives and children. If the hospital is bombed, we will be unable to help you. If you find another place for the radio, you can have your station and the hospital too. Isn't that better than taking this risk?"

The visitors talked among themselves a few moments, agreed that it was, then left.

Eight days later three American diplomats drove in from the north. They reported the Pak army had Chittagong under control, but there was still much fighting in the countryside. The consulate felt very strongly that nonessential personnel at the hospital should evacuate. They would escort them back to a ship in Chittagong.

The majority of the Malumghat team declined the offer. But two couples with young children and two single women accepted the escort. It was time for their furlough and their colleagues encouraged them to go ahead and take the last ship out. When one of the diplomats said they wouldn't be back, Dr. Ketcham asked if there wasn't some way the hospital group could be kept informed. "Listen to the Voice of America news," one of the men advised.

The following Wednesday evening, after a tiring day of assisting in surgery, nurse Rebecca Davy switched on her bedside radio at 11:15 P.M., though she rarely listened to the radio. She heard a voice saying, "This is a special message from Washington to the Americans at Malumghat, East Pakistan. The road to Chittagong is now closed. All nonessential personnel should leave through Burma immediately." Miss Davy alerted the group and everyone began packing. Usually the power station thirty miles away switched off the electricity at 10 P.M. This night the lights burned until 4 A.M., facilitating packing.

At eight in the morning four jeep loads of missionaries and children sped south. Vic Olsen remained at the hospital.

Donn Ketcham drove one of the jeeps to the Burma border, saw the evacuees off in a rented sampan, and started back.

The hasty departure had alarmed the hospital's staff of sixty nationals. Vic Olsen called them together and was trying to calm their fears when a loud boom shook the ground. The result was instant confusion as everyone dived under tables and benches. When they realized it was only thunder, they got up laughing at their own jumpiness.

There was much reason for concern. The "bamboo telegraph" reported rebels digging in about a mile north to confront the advancing Pak army moving down from Chittagong. Donn Ketcham returned and said he had passed through several rebel checkpoints on the road south.

Since opening in 1966, only once had the hospital been closed—this when a rare type of hepatitis had bedded almost the entire foreign staff for three months. They had kept it open even when inundated by a cholera epidemic of six hundred cases. A team of doctors from the U.S. AID financed Cholera Research Hospital in Dacca had handled the overflow in a tent. But now Dr. Olsen and Dr. Ketcham felt the staff and ambulatory patients should be sent to safe haven. They would remain to care for injured, help their Bengali friends, and try to protect the valuable hospital and equipment.

During the busy day of closing, Vic Olsen took a bad spill on his Honda cycle. A hurried X-ray revealed what he felt: a fractured right elbow. Sustained only by aspirin and a sling, he went back to work. Not until that night did he stretch out on the operating table and submit to anesthesia. Dr. Ketcham operated and inserted a steel pin and after a sedated night's sleep the patient was back at work.

For years a few antagonists of the Christian faith in the area had spread tales that the Abwey missionaries were CIA agents in disguise. Now the doctors heard that the rumor mills were claiming the American "agents" had been instructed by the "imperialist" Voice of America.

Their feelings of insecurity increased when a Bengali friend came to warn them they would be hit by bandits after the lights went out at ten. That night Donn Ketcham dozed at the hospital with a shotgun between his knees. His partner took up position on a mattress behind the door of his home. Vic Olsen's right elbow throbbed and his left hand held a revolver. The lights stayed on again miraculously—all night this time!

The next day Donn Ketcham carried his shotgun out to a single-lane road that ran near the hospital. In full view of a crowd of Bengalis he took careful aim at a mangy stray dog and pulled the trigger. "Just to show them the shotgun is loaded," he told Vic Olsen when he returned to the hospital."

Several days later a long column of Pak army vehicles rolled in from the north. The doctors met the steely-faced commander.

"Why have you been treating our enemies?" the Pak officer summarily demanded.

Donn Ketcham did not pull punches. "Major, you have your military code. We respect that. We Christian physicians have our code. It calls for us to help anyone hurt or sick regardless of politics or religion. We'll help you and your men just as we'll help the local people. You may be needing us," he added with a quick smile.

The mustached Punjabi said nothing.

"So will you guarantee the safety of our hospital staff?" Dr. Ketcham asked.

"Yes," the officer agreed. "We need the hospital operating."

"We also have Hindus on our staff. Will you guarantee their

safety, too?" asked Dr. Olsen.

The Muslim soldier frowned, but said he would.

Dr. Olsen then took the calculated risk and pleaded for the lives of all the Hindus of the area. Now angry, the Pak commander only said, "We'll see." Then he turned on his heels, strode to his jeep and roared off to the south.

Believing that the hospital could continue operating, the doctors sent word for the employees to return. But some had already fled to India.

With a partial staff and within the limits of their strengths, Vic Olsen and Donn Ketcham did all they could to fulfill the demands of their code. As they worked, they wondered how their families and the other evacuees were faring.

By this time Chittagong was as barren of people as Dacca. All Protestant missionaries had left except Reid Minich and a British Baptist couple.

Gordon and Nesta Soddy had served in East Pakistan since 1933. Gordon, a six-foot four-inch, husky Oxford man and classmate of Leslie Wenger, was secretary of the twenty-seven member British Baptist mission in East Pakistan. From their house that straddled a small steep hill, the Soddys watched fighting around a tennis court below. The combatants withdrew leaving two dead on the court. After a couple of days the Soddys saw crows picking at the corpses.

The gunfire and explosions coming from the business district discouraged them from trying to cross town to reach the Bengali Baptist church where they worshiped. They could walk to the new red brick Assemblies of God church at the foot of the hill. On Sundays in March Gordon conducted services there in place of Josephine Spina, the church's buxom missionary lady minister who had left on one of the evacuation ships.

On Wednesday, March 31, the Soddys took in their first

refugees. Two Catholic priests came in a little Volkswagen bringing three young women. "They were staying at the medical college hospital," one priest explained. "We had to get them out when the military moved into the nurses' quarters. The pregnant girl and this young woman are sisters."

Before either of the Soddys could ask who the third young woman was, the sister of the expectant mother said, "Please. We brought a midwife."

About 9:30 the next morning, between sporadic bursts of distant gunfire, a newborn's lusty cry sounded a note of hope. They named her Rebecca and Gordon Soddy led in a prayer of dedication.

IV

Freedom's Flickering Light

THAT THE BENGALIS seemed not to have learned their lesson enraged Tikka Khan. He ordered his military commander to smash the resistance before the June monsoons put half the country under water. He knew that the Muktis would be harder to snare then.

This meant going after the elusive guerillas who had melted into the countryside.

One group of "Freedom Brothers" had found haven in villages around the British Baptist hospital at Chondragona, forty miles north of Chittagong. The army came after them in late April.

The British missionaries moved their families and national staff into the 130-bed hospital when the first firefights erupted. The influx of extra people added to the patients taxed the hospital from the start. But as wounded guerillas and villagers were brought in, food supplies dwindled and their plight became critical. With a constantly increasing population they could not even get out to bury the dead.

They were down to one meal a day when the army broke

through. The Pak commander angrily confronted the British doctor, Dr. Bryan Whitty. "Why didn't you leave with the other foreigners?" he demanded. "Why are you helping enemies of the state?"

Dr. Whitty responded as had Dr. Olsen. "God called us here to help the sick and injured. That includes everyone. If you have wounded men, bring them in. We'll treat them with the other patients."

The Pak officer was not anxious to start an incident with a British national. He backed down and even permitted food supplies to be brought in.

Feni, thirty miles farther north where the McKinley family lived, was still under Mukti control. The guerillas had blown up bridges and felled trees and dug ditches across the roads leading into the town.

Jim McKinley moved freely around the heavily Muslim town. Freedom Brothers greeted him cheerily, for his service to the cyclone sufferers was well known. Jim counseled and prayed with Muktis and others and gave relief money to families in special need. He listened to their complaints about Pakistani oppression, but maintained a quiet neutrality.

At 5:30 P.M., Tuesday, April 6, his heart turned to the Bengali cause.

Thirteen-year-old Cherry first saw the two "strange-looking planes" flying low. Instinctively she pulled her two younger brothers to the ground as the Saber Jets roared past, spewing bullets ahead into the crowded marketplace.

Five times the planes came back, spitting death at screaming civilians. The McKinleys and their four children were not harmed, but they could hear the shrieks of the wounded and dying. "Stay here," Jim told his family after the planes were gone. "I'm going to the marketplace."

He found the streets around the produce stalls littered with dead and wounded. Stricken with shock and outrage, he pitched in to help get the wounded to the local hospital. He handled babies with bodies torn apart; old grandmothers with faces like raw, cut tomatoes. He had never believed it possible, but the carnage seemed worse than the aftermath of the cyclone.

He worked until his arms felt ready to fall off. Benumbed and stained with Bengali blood, he staggered home to a questioning family. It was hard to talk without terrifying the children, but he tried. When he finished, Cherry's heart-shaped face wore a haunting look he would never forget. "Why, Daddy?" she whispered in unbelief. "Why?"

He lifted his drooping chin and looked into her bewildered blue eyes. "Because," he said in a surprisingly strong voice, "the Bengalis want their independence. They want freedom as Americans did during our revolution."

The McKinleys could hear the people rushing by on the road outside now. They were fleeing as thousands of Bengalis in other towns had already done. Jim and Betty sat and talked quietly with their children, groping for words to assure them that God was on the side of the innocent, that justice would ultimately prevail.

All night and the next day and night people poured past. Then the planes roared back to complete the destruction of downtown Feni. Within a day of this second attack the town was deserted.

At 6 A.M. after the second strafing the McKinleys piled luggage into five hired cycle rickshaws and started walking behind. Travelers along the road saw them and shouted, *"Joi Bangla!" "Joi Bangla!"* the McKinleys called back sincerely.

They made forty miles the first day and slept in a deserted Baptist mission house at Comilla. The next morning they

started again and ran into an artillery barrage. Most of the
refugees were turning to enter India barely five miles away.
Though the ground was shaking, the McKinleys decided to
try for Dacca. "If we go to India, we might never get back,"
Jim said.

About ten miles from the capital, they reached a ferry
where Pak soldiers were unloading cartons of ammunition. What they saw chilled their blood. Each box was
stamped with the familiar handshake symbol of U.S. AID and
marked "Gift from the People of the U.S.A. to the People of
Pakistan."

They transferred to two taxis on the far side of the river
and reached their mission house at 5:30. Only two servants
were there to greet them. They unpacked and settled in.

Jim and Betty worried how the past week's experience
would affect their children. They had brought thirteen-year-
old Cherry, the oldest, to this country when she was only
nine months old. All the children had grown up with the
Bengalis, speaking their language, absorbing their aspira-
tions for freedom. Would they be scarred by bitterness
against the Pak government and army?

They caught Cherry's feelings from a poem she wrote a
few nights after their arrival in Dacca.

Roaring out of the Bengal sunset they came
Two black dots on a warm summer evening
Some children stopped their playing to
Set clear eyes upon them.
In awe watching the pair
Soaring over rice fields and straw huts
Like finches looking for someplace to rest their wings.
But suddenly as they spotted the tiny town
Their nature changed and now like vultures
They screech and get down upon it

A piercing wail rings out and then
Boom, Boom, Boom.
The children scatter like frightened ants into their homes
Amid the constant shattering blasts
Flinging themselves upon the floor
They lay frozen in fear
Their faces ghastly, their blood cold, their heads lined,
Buzzing with the question—Why?
While outside the vultures peck at their prize.
A mother tries to comfort a whimpering child with
    shaking hands.
The only steady comforting sound is the thunk, thunk of the
    father's feet pacing the floor.
Again and again the planes dip and
Again and again
Boom, Boom, Boom.
In the same mysterious way they appeared
They are gone.
All is quiet.
The world seems dead . . . off in the distance
Comes the clattering of wheels on the old road
And the jingling of bells like water from a broken dam.
The living gush into the countryside
Trying to escape from the smell of death and blood.
Some cry, some with faces of white stone plod along together
Not saying a word.
Not having to because their grief is written on their faces.
Slowly they all filter away.
Night comes, the stars twinkle, a cool breeze flows from
    the south.
The only irritating sound is the crickets which seem to say
Love your enemies, love your enemies, love your enemies.

The next evening they heard a jeep pull up and a gravel
voice call, "Anybody home?"

At their response Mark Tucker strolled in and asked casually, "Got anything to eat? My wife has left me and I'm hungry for some good southern cooking."

Mark updated them on Dacca news. "Two of your couples have left. The Parshalls and the Olsons may be the only Protestants still here. We're keeping the Cholera Hospital open. No matter what, you have cholera always in this country."

Mark continued, "And, say, if you must go out at night drive with your dome lights on and stop any time you see a shadow move. These sentries are like neighborhood dogs. If one sees something and fires, the guy down the street will fire too."

Had Mark heard news of the Carl Rhythers and Tom Thurmans, two Southern Baptist couples stationed in Faridpur, fifty miles west? "No, but people coming into our hospital say there's a lot of fighting up north where the Australian Baptists are with the Garo tribespeople. And around Doc Gilbert's Church of God hospital at Bogra."

Jim McKinley sighed. "Well, let's hope and pray they are safe or got out to India."

While the McKinleys and Tucker talked, the Thurman and Rhyther families were sheltered in their mission house on the western side of the broad Ganges River. Their model farm and industrial center had been disrupted by reports of troop movements. Now they could hear low rumbles in the distance. They didn't think it was thunder.

At breakfast the next morning sudden *boom . . . booms* sent them dashing to an inner bedroom. A mortar fell on the mission workshop about three hundred yards away, followed by heavy rifle firing. They lay flat on the floor for an hour while stray bullets whined about the house.

That night the guns were silent, but the sky in all directions glowed red from blazing buildings.

Soldiers stomped into the house the next morning searching for guns. They found none and left.

The following Saturday night a very pregnant young Bengali woman pounded on the door. For three days she had run from rapacious soldiers. The missionaries invited her to join about forty other Bengalis who had taken refuge with them. "Better get our emergency medical manual out, Gloria," Tom Thurman, a drawling Mississippian, advised his wife. "She looks about ready to pop."

Sunday morning her labor pains started and in the afternoon Gloria assisted in the delivery of a healthy baby boy. They named him Samson.

The main Pak force moved on, with a residual of soldiers remaining to keep control. The departing troops carried with them a screaming, kicking selection of Bengali girls. They left behind acres of ashes, scores of wounded and dead, and grieving relatives. Under cover of night many of those able to walk struck out for India.

The sky darkened and torrents of premonsoon water soaked the ashes. "Even the sky is weeping," a sorrowing Bengali told the missionaries.

The Thurmans and Rhythers did what they could to help. After ten days they felt their children needed a change. They traveled in a small boat down the broad Ganges for nine hours, then crossed to the east and boarded a bus bound for Dacca. The McKinleys were glad to have company.

A few days later Dr. Vic Olsen, his arm still in a sling, drove in from the south and shared his experiences. He was hoping to get news of his family and the other Abwey evacuees that had left through Burma.

On a hunch he went to the airport for the arrival of a Thai International flight from Bangkok. To his happy surprise, he saw his petite wife, Joan, leading their two younger children off the plane. (Two older children were attending high school in West Pakistan.) Kitty Ketcham and about half of the others were behind Joan.

The doctor forgot the cultural taboo against a man showing affection to his wife in public. He ran and embraced Joan joyfully. "We had to buy tickets all the way to Karachi," Joan said after the embrace. "They let us off here to clear customs while they refuel. We'll have to get back on in a half hour for we have no permit to enter East Pakistan. But what happened to your arm?"

He told her quickly for he wanted to know how she and the others had fared.

"Well! After crossing in that flimsy sampan we slept the first night on the floor at a customs station. No sleeping bags or pillows. Then we were shuttled in old trucks to a river port where we boarded a rusty old ship. It ran aground near the sea and we spent that night on the ship. Finally a Burmese navy ship came to the rescue and carried us to Akyab. We took a chartered flight to Rangoon and from there flew to Bangkok. Finally our Pakistan visas were granted, but the embassy said we couldn't return to East Pakistan due to the rebellion. We're on our way to West Pakistan to be with Lynn and Wendy and the other high school kids. I do hope we get there in time for Wendy's graduation. But how is life at the hospital?"

Vic smiled. "We have lots of patients and refugees, but there's been no shooting close by. We persuaded the local Pak commander that it was in his best interest to leave the villages around the hospital alone. But a lot of homes have been burned by bandit elements."

"I wish we could go back with you," Joan said wistfully. "But I suppose—"

Her husband snapped his fingers in interruption. "Maybe

there is. I know a few people here. Wait for me."

He hurried away and in a few moments returned grinning. "You have permission to go with me to the hospital for tonight. We'll pack and go back together for Wendy's graduation. And since the fighting seems to have quieted down, perhaps we could go on to the States for our furlough."

"Let's go, then," Joan said impatiently. "That's wonderful."

But as the Olsens and their friends left for the pocket of relative peace around the Malumghat Hospital, missionaries in the north were experiencing extreme difficulties.

At Pabna, northwest of Dacca, two Australian Baptist couples, the Stuart Robinsons and the Jeff Ryals, escaped just ahead of Pak mortars. They crossed a river on a crude raft of roped-together poles and walked seventy-five miles to India. At Brahanbaria, northeast of the capital, a New Zealand Baptist couple and two single girls escaped a battle and walked fifteen miles to India. In the far north, a Scandinavian Lutheran family and a British Baptist couple also fled to India in a hurry. All had to leave what belongings they could not carry for looters.

Dr. Eva Gilbert, the senior missionary in the north, was not about to leave the Church of God hospital at Bogra where she had served for forty years. "I have another year before retirement," she told her staff. "I can stay until then."

Ordinarily a pleasant woman, Dr. Gilbert had her dander up. She was angry over reports of killing and raping by Pak soldiers. She faced the Pak officer with a stony gaze and declared, "We don't approve of what your men are doing."

The officer hemmed and hawed and moved his feet nervously as he tried to state his case.

"Well, we're going to treat the sick and wounded," she finally said. "Will you honor our neutrality?"

"Your hospital and church will not be bothered by us," he promised.

"Very well. And if your soldiers can act like gentlemen, they are welcome to attend our services."

"I'll tell my men. A few are Christians and may want to come."

A few Sundays later a uniformed Pak officer came to Dr. Gilbert's church and sat with head down during the service. At the end he asked to speak.

"Some of us went to Christian mission schools in the west," the tall Punjabi recalled. "We believe in Jesus Christ and helping people as you do." He twisted uneasily and looked away. A sob burst in his throat. "We—we're being forced to do these awful things. God forgive us." He was unable to continue.

A few Christian soldiers from the west were attending churches in other cities where the Mukti had been driven out. They also came fully uniformed, bearing rifles. They seldom smiled and frequently cried during services.

The major cities now lay in an uneasy calm. Most of the Hindus and many Muslims had left for India. A hundred thousand a day were pouring across the border in May and straggling into hastily improvised refugee camps. By the end of the month the Indian government had counted over four million refugees.

Most Bengali Christians were staying home. It seemed that the Pak army's fury was aimed at Hindus and at Muslims who sympathized with the independence movement. Christian houses and churches were not being burned.

This was so strongly believed that many Hindus crowded into churches and mission stations begging for instant conversion.

Catholic and Protestant missionaries and national pastors

all declined to administer quick baptisms. They admitted the serious to classes and helped them memorize Scripture portions such as the Lord's Prayer and the Ten Commandments. In some localities such knowledge saved the lives of some Hindus who were brought before firing squads. Crosses worn around the neck and the sign Christian House on Hindu dwellings also helped.

The missionaries felt they were also relatively safe. The Pak government seemed acutely concerned about world opinion and protested "exaggerated" press reports of military brutality. Tikka Khan even invited in a few foreign journalists to take a guided tour. "We have been maligned," he told them. "The army has saved the country, not destroyed it. We want only perfect law and order."

Army tour guides showed the journalists a well choked with skeletons. "Enemies of the state acting in conspiracy with India did this," the guides claimed.

But *Time*'s Louis Kraar managed to slip away from the tour to a devastated Hindu section. As he walked across rubble and ashes, a young Bengali student ran up and whispered, "Until today, when you came, they have been killing people."

The foreign missionaries were not taken in by government pretensions of innocence. But except for smuggling out occasional letters, they were helpless. To protest publicly would only result in deportation.

Among themselves they smiled ironically at slanted newspaper stories and television broadcasts. One night at the Southern Baptist mission house in Dacca the McKinleys, Thurmans, Parshalls, and Troy Bennetts (a Baptist family just returned from furlough) were watching President Yahya Khan tell a news conference that "everything was under control." Suddenly a gun battle erupted in the streets outside. They fell to the floor to escape whizzing bullets. When the firing stopped they got up laughing at the absurdity of it all.

But the chilling news that came from the Catholic archbishop's office was no laughing matter.

Italian Father Mario Veronese had been in the Catholic mission hospital at Jessore, about 150 miles southwest of Dacca, when he saw soldiers coming. Hoping to stop trouble, he came out with his hands up. He did not have a cassock on, but the Red Cross symbol on his arm was clearly visible. Shots rang out. The soldiers stepped over his dead body and ran through the hospital shooting staff members running along corridors. A missionary who escaped managed to return and take pictures of the slain missionary. He showed these to local civil authorities and received profuse apologies and a plea that it was a mistake. Nothing about the incident was printed in the newspapers.

While the small foreign mission community in Dacca was still absorbing this report, a second "mistake" was made.

After tea with Italian Father Lucas in his apartment at Ruhea in the far north, visiting soldiers rewarded his hospitality by a severe beating with a tire iron. He crawled to the road and asked a cart driver to take him across the border to India less than five miles away. He was dead on arrival.

V

The Smugglers

UNTIL MAY 14 Father Ed Goedert, a lean, wry-faced Holy
Cross missionary from Oak Park, Illinois, thought the stories
of Pak atrocities highly overestimated. But Father Goedert
hadn't been to Dacca in four months. He had no telephone.
And, though his St. Nicholas parish at Nagari village was only
twenty-five miles north of Dacca, he could be reached during
the dry season only along a narrow path.

His church was in a mango grove at the tail end of a string
of villages sometimes called the Catholic "holy land" of Bangladesh. Catholic faith had been planted in the area by Por-
tuguese priests in 1695 and had grown to include fourteen
thousand faithful in thirty square miles of fertile rice and jute
fields. The keynote of church extension was education. Father Goedert's Nagari school alone had twelve hundred
beaming, brown-faced Bengalis enrolled.

On the fateful Friday afternoon of the fourteenth the children at Nagari were impatiently waiting for the closing bell
when popping sounds like exploding firecrackers floated
across the fields.

Curious but not anxious, Father Goedert looked in the direction of Baira, a Hindu village. He saw tongues of flame darting above the tops of mango trees that shaded the bamboo huts of Baira. He hurriedly called his Bengali assistant, Father Benjamin Costa, and pointed out the flames. "The war is coming to us. Send the children home."

A half hour later the first refugees straggled up the trail, wide-eyed in fear and carrying pitifully small bundles of possessions. "Soldiers! Shooting, burning!" they gasped. "Help us."

The two priests and the teaching sisters and brothers opened up the classrooms.

After dark the first wounded were brought in. Father Goedert looked down at a wisp of a girl, comatose with a bullet in her head. Her brother lay beside her screaming with a shattered leg. Their mother was dead. Local medics, poorly trained by American standards, had never seen bullet wounds. Working without pain-deadening anesthetics, they stitched wounds far into the night. Father Goedert assisted, muttering, "From now on I can believe anything."

For a terror-filled week the soldiers marched from one Hindu village to another, searching for Mukti Bahini, gunning down fleeing civilians, grabbing girls, firing the bamboo homes. Every day Father Goedert and his assistants received hundreds of frightened refugees, many of them wounded. They had left their dead behind, afraid to take time for burial. By the twenty-first they were feeding by actual count 10,407 refugees. Of these, 4,155 were jammed into the school buildings and the rest were taken into the humble homes of Nagari Catholics.

Father Goedert quickly expended the church's relief supplies and emptied the treasury for money to buy more. He had heard that CORR was continuing the cyclone relief program and dispatched a letter to Dacca.

> We have so many problems that, at times, we even forget
> to be afraid. One bullet case has died. He has the distinction
> of being the only Hindu to be buried in our cemetery in 280
> years, though he probably does not appreciate it. . . . We have
> had five deliveries, one case of typhoid, and hundreds of dys-
> entery. We need everything: food, clothes, medicine; and we
> need it yesterday.

CORR never answered the letter, but smuggled out a bag
of money with instructions to survey the devastated villages.
Father Goedert dispatched runners to buy food and medicines in the nearest towns and began compiling a grim tally.
He reported to CORR:

> The condition in Baira is appalling. Forty-nine people dead,
> and the number is rising; 174 homes totally destroyed; 86
> more partially destroyed; about 500 tons of rice, their entire
> food supply for the year either burned or stolen. Most of them
> have only the one piece of clothing that they fled in, bled in
> and sweat in since May 14th.
> We can't help them rebuild their homes now. The Army
> might return next week and re-destroy them. But we can give
> them food and clothes and hope. So . . . we intend to go ahead.
> We're bucking the government and we're scared stiff. But we
> have God on our side, even though He hasn't exactly been
> overdoing it lately.

In mid-June he wrote CORR:

> For those of us who only watch, it is impossible to keep the
> hatred from rising out of our hearts to our lips. What then
> must it be for those who are suffering? We now have 26
> devastated villages on our list for surveying. The Army de-

stroyed only five of these; the others were looted or destroyed by their Muslim neighbors. Good Muslims who try to stop these Judases find themselves in trouble.

Each day people come with their pitiful pleas for help. One woman with four little children and a fifth obviously on the way asks us to find her husband. The Army took him away and she has no news of him at all. As she was crying out her story, a man was patiently waiting. The Army had lined up and shot the young men of his village. His two sons were killed, and his 12-year-old daughter abducted. . . . He knew we could not give him back his sons, but could we do something to get his daughter back? No wonder people finally decide to fight. I wonder if the Liberation Army will accept a 53-year-old volunteer with a bad stomach and a worse disposition.

While Father Goedert was undergoing his baptism into the Bengali cause, Yahya Khan grandly announced he would transfer power to the elected representatives "in three or four months." Meanwhile a group of appointed experts would write the new constitution. "The army," he bragged, "is in full control of the situation in the east."

This was hardly true. The Muktis had retreated from the cities to engage in guerilla warfare. The Freedom Brothers were blowing up bridges, dynamiting ferries and trains, toppling radio towers by cutting thick guy wires with hacksaws. Their mobile transmitters broadcast a continual flow of independence songs, speeches, and pledges of loyalty to jailed Sheik Mujib. Mimeographed "freedom" communiqués traveled faster than the regular mail. Newsboys even slipped Mukti reports into government newspapers hawked on the streets of Dacca and Chittagong.

By July, seven million Bengalis had crossed the border into India. World sympathy was turning toward the Bengalis. Washington had been pressured to stop arms shipments to the Khan regime. But to the consternation of the American missionaries, the Nixon administration still seemed to favor Yahya Khan. *Newsweek* quoted one U.S. diplomat as saying, "We are more interested in stability than morality at the moment. . . . Right now the chance for stability, slim as it is, seems to lie with Yahya."*

"I still sing 'God Bless America,' " Father Goedert wrote CORR in Dacca, "although these sentiments definitely do not apply to the administration." And again, "Our poor people can't understand the American logic which allows an American president to help kill them while the American people are helping keep them alive. No wonder they think all foreigners are nuts."

President Nixon's surprise July fifteenth announcement that he would visit Red China seemed to let the cat out of the mysterious diplomatic bag of relations with Pakistan. Apparently the Pak government had helped to set up Henry Kissinger's trip that resulted in the invitation. But this was no balm to the besieged Bengalis and their missionary friends.

On the rainy morning of the twenty-fifth Father Goedert was ending 6 o'clock mass when an explosion shook the church. He ran outside to learn that the Muktis had blown up a train on the track that ran about three-fourths of a mile away.

He called a Bengali doctor to help the injured. The doctor refused to go alone, so Father Goedert commandeered a boat. The heavy monsoons had pushed water within fifteen feet of the church.

A Bengali oarsman rowed them toward the wreck. From about two hundred yards they saw an army train pulling in from behind. The terrified boatman whipped his craft

*August 2, 1971, p. 28.

around and started back. But soldiers had seen them and opened fire as they leaped into the water.

With bullets spraying the water behind them, Father Goedert and the doctor swam frantically toward high ground. Exhausted and near drowning, the priest called for help. Fortunately the boatman had held on to the boat. He pulled the boat over and pulled the priest aboard. All three got to shore safely.

That afternoon the army began putting Christian villages in the area to the torch. Most people fled ahead of the vengeful arsonists, but in Dori Para village a Christian father of ten and an old man too sick to run were killed.

Three days later Father Goedert was upstairs in his rectory recounting his narrow escape the previous Sunday.

In the space of 20 agonizing minutes, I became a Bengali, devised a new language and revised my theology. I became a Bengali because now I have shared with them the sheer panic and terror of fleeing for my life, defenseless, and unable to hide or fight back. I devised a new language because neither my American English nor my Bengali was adequate to express my opinion of the barbarian Pakistan Army, my thoughts regarding their origin and my hopes for their future. I revised my theology on the grounds that this business about loving your enemy needs rethinking. It was based originally on the supposition that the enemy is human.

While slipping the note to CORR into an envelope, he heard the sound of a mass movement of people. He rushed downstairs just in time to see the last of the thousands of refugees fleeing into the bush. His ear caught the chug of a motor and then he saw the reason for the alarm. The boat contained soldiers manning machine guns pointed at the rectory. Flanked by his Bengali assistant, Father Benjamin Costa, and three visiting American mis-

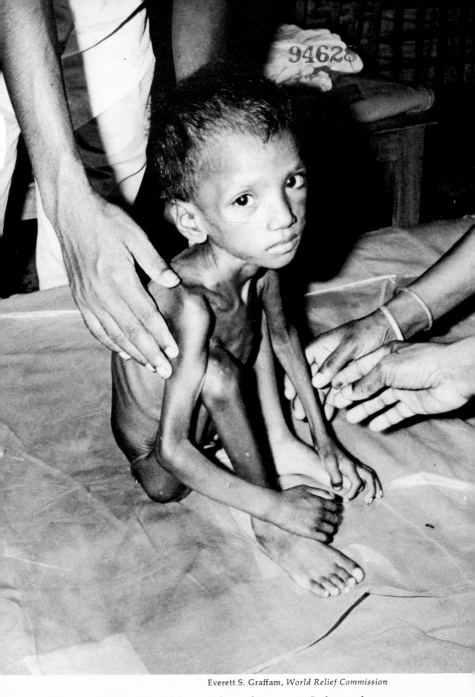

94628

Everett S. Graffam, *World Relief Commission*

Pictures of Bengali children such as this one in Indian refugee camps stirred the conscience of the world.

Veteran Assemblies of God missionary Calvin Olson views evidence of the "lesson" taught by the Pakistan Army on the night of March 25, 1971.

After the Instrument of Surrender was signed, die-hard, fanatical Muslims slaughtered Bengali intellectuals in a last dash of carnage.

Sheikh Mujib Rahman, a Muslim, has shown warm appreciation for Christian aid. The Prime Minister (center) here receives a gift copy of *The Living Bible* from Dr. Viggo Olsen (left) and Dr. Ray Knighton, representing Medical Assistance Programs.

The plight of the refugees touched the world's heart. Here Msgr. Robert J. Hagarty of Chicago (center) helps check cargo for a Catholic Relief Services emergency airlift of aid supplies flown from New York to Calcutta on November 4, 1971. With Msgr. Hagarty at JFK International Airport are Rev. Joseph J. Walter (left), Director of the Catholic Medical Mission Board, and Msgr. Andrew P. Landi of Catholic Relief Services.

Two Wheaton College members of the Bangladesh Brigade—Bob Purdy (left), freshman from New York; and Don Lemon, freshman son of Vietnam missionary parents—pause before one of the bamboo houses just completed. The 21 Brigaders were responsible for building or repairing 10,000 houses under a U.S. AID grant.

CORR high yield rice project at Baniarchock in Faridput District.

Under a CORR program called "test relief," unemployed Bengalis are paid a wage of about forty cents a day to build roads, levees, and similar projects. Here workers carry dirt to elevate marshy church property.

Widow paid by CORR to clean wheat before milling.

Leprosy victim trained in tailoring by CORR.

J.D. Hughey, *Foreign Mission Board, Southern Baptist Convention*

After the "storm of the century," which took a toll of a half million lives, polluted water endangered survivors. Here Southern Baptist's Jim McKinley and Bengali assistants sink a "tube" well in the marshy delta.

Transport is a problem in a land laced with waterways. The elephant works for Bangladesh Ecumenical Relief and Rehabilitation Service. BEERS is funded by councils of Protestant churches in various countries and Church World Service in the U.S.

BEERS

Partnership Mission

ABWE

Because of British influences, almost all educated people in Bangladesh read and speak English. Rochunga Pudaite, Indian head of Partnership Mission, stands by stacks of *Living New Testament* bound for Bangladesh. Partnership Mission is mailing a New Testament to every person with a telephone.

High government officials come from Dacca, over 250 miles away, to seek medical help at the Muhlumghat Christian Memorial Hospital operated by the Association of Baptists for World Evangelism.

Catholic Archbishop Ganguly and happy well-fed children greet authors at Tumilia mission station.

James Hefley

James Hefley

Still unsolved is the Bihari problem. The million-and-a-half ethnic minority aided the Pakistan Army during the struggle for independence and now fear revenge from the majority Bengalis. These two women once enjoyed privilege; now they are quartered in a Bihari camp outside of Dacca.

sionary brothers, he walked to the water's edge.

"I hope you come in peace," he said without emotion.

The officer in command replied, "Yes, but we heard you have guerillas."

"We had old people, women, and children. They fled."

"Why did they run if they're innocent?" the Pak asked.

Father Goedert curled his lip and replied acidly. "I fled when the army shot at me."

The officer was not amused. He and his men searched the rectory, church, and school. Then after warning them not to harbor "enemies of the state," they left.

The refugees returned after the army boat left. Some told Father Goedert they had hidden under water sucking air through hollow reeds.

More kept coming. By the end of August Father Goedert and his staff were caring for upwards of fifteen thousand refugees. He had to drastically increase his smuggled orders to CORR.

An administrator in CORR's Dacca office saw the enlarged request and whistled. He gave the money to the underground courier, but added a note asking Father Goedert to send a detailed explanation of why he needed so much money.

Father Goedert replied testily:

> We need money because people are hungry, clothes because some are in rags and medicine because they are sick. What other reasons can you give?
>
> We have received several more warnings to stop helping anti-state elements—which is the Pakistani word for refugees. Knowing of the wholesale slaughter that has occurred in other places, we live in fear. Each morning we wonder what the day will bring; each night we marvel that we are still alive.

The lean Father Goedert, who was steadily losing weight, was only one of many missionaries involved in "anti-state" activities to save lives during the long wet summer of 1971.

There was Father Rignon at Jalipur near Dacca. He told frightened Hindus they could say they were Christians. He taught them prayers, how to make the sign of the cross, and passed out crosses. When his supply of crosses were exhausted, he taught them to make their own from foil inside cigarette boxes. But when the soldiers came through looking for Hindus, one youth recanted and said, "I cannot lie. I am a Hindu." He was bayoneted to death for his honesty.

Near Dinajpur in the far north the Army killed 175 people in one village as a punishment for the slaying of seven soldiers. Italian Father Sciavi complained bitterly to the colonel in charge about the shootings, mentioning that three of his parishioners had been shot. The officer retorted, "We should have killed three hundred." A nearby village was not touched by the army, apparently because the soldiers feared contagion from the Catholic leprosarium there.

Near hard-hit Mymensingh, Italian Fathers Homrich and Trippi and two Italian nuns operated a relief program twice as large as Father Goedert's with money smuggled out from CORR. Most of their refugees were Hindus hiding in the adjoining forty-square mile Madhupur Forest. The missionaries also took in about one hundred local girls, mostly Hindus, as "novices," according to Father Homrich, "to protect them from the soldiers and help some of the girls stay girls." Whenever Pak soldiers came sniffing around he would say, "If you try to harm them you'll have to shoot me first." What the army did not know was that Father Homrich was a Mukti Bahini chaplain and his house was a guerilla headquarters.

Stepped up guerilla activity kept the Nagari area a hot spot. Pak officials warned Archbishop Ganguly that continuing "anti-state" activities by Father Goedert and other priests were endangering the work of all Catholic missionaries in the country. The Bengali churchman listened, then said quietly, "I am sure Father Goedert and other priests are only helping poor people."

The archbishop had already taken the precaution of sending most of his Bengali clergy staff to country parishes. He himself frequently traveled about his diocese giving encouragement to the people. On trips he was always careful to take one or more foreign priests with him.

On one trip he was returning from Mymensingh in the northeast to Dacca with a Britisher and two Americans. About dark they were halted at military roadblocks.

"Identity cards! License!" a rough voice shouted. They handed over the proper papers.

The soldiers peered at Archbishop Ganguly's card, then stepped back for a conference. He caught the words, "foreigners . . . let them go."

He drove away convinced the missionaries had saved his life.

The evangelical missionaries matched the Catholics in their dedication to mercy. Through the summer they continued receiving refugees, especially girls. They kept those they could and helped others escape to India. It was common knowledge now that Pak soldiers were kidnaping hundreds of girls for sex slaves in their encampments.

The evangelicals also smuggled or carried relief money to communities in special distress. Beside soldiers, there was the danger on such trips of being robbed by Bihari collaborators called *razakars* who also kidnaped girls for the military. Once, for example, Adventist Jabil Jacobs was ordered over to the river bank by armed *razakars*. He had a bag of money for seven village churches who were giving relief to Hindus.

His boatman shouted back, "No. We are Christians just passing through." He then pulled back the throttle and raced away in a dash of spray.

Bishop Blair, the Anglican prelate of Dacca, was not quite so fortunate on a trip to Barisal. He was stopped, searched, and relieved of thirty rupees (about $4.25). But they missed a thick stack of bills tucked in a pocket under his cassock.

The monsoons slackened and the water began receding in September. There were now Christians in the Mukti Bahini and the military knew it. Official hints were dropped that government patience was growing short. The army would not protect subversives masquerading as Christians from the wrath of "patriotic elements" (Bihari collaborators).

Fresh reports indicated that this was true.

At Bogra a Bihari band invaded the home of a respected Christian teacher of the Church of God, Utpal Biswas, who was too sick to flee. They killed him, his wife, daughter (a nurse at Dr. Gilbert's hospital) and two sons. At Muladi village near Barisal in the south, five Christians were killed and their homes burned. In Father Goedert's area Christians were now considered fair game by soldiers trying to suppress the slippery Muktis.

The pressure was being felt in the far south. The Army had continued its policy of not raiding villages around the Abwey hospital. But *razakars* and other bandits had been burning and looting Hindu homes in increasing numbers.

Donn Ketcham caught about sixty men plundering the house of a village merchant who had fled to India. He chased them out and hired movers to take the absent family's belongings to the hospital's warehouse for safekeeping. Another time Jay Walsh and Dr. Ketcham called three Pak officers in to look at a dying Hindu goldsmith, horribly disfigured from acid poured over his face. "This is what your friends did to a man trying to protect his daughter," the missionaries said icily. "Can't you stop them?" They promised to try.

The hospital had kept a relief program going since April. In September the lines of hungry peasants grew longer than the food supply. Some fell down before Dr. Ketcham, locking their arms around his legs and begging for help. One hollow-faced farmer, when told there was no more food that day, shrieked, "Then show me where to die."

But the times were also trying in the swelling refugee camps across the border. Here, except for freedom from fear of attack, conditions were almost as bad.

VI

Acres of Agony

HOUSES BURNED, daughters raped, young men killed, the refugees swam and padded barefoot into India by the millions. Mothers in torn, muddy saris carried babies too weak to cry. Old men hobbled across leading hollow-eyed, starving children. Fathers rowed boats, pedaled rickshaws, pushed carts bulging with family belongings. Many of the homeless arrived pocked with sores, often smallpox. Some reached the border in a last-gasp effort, collapsed in their tracks, and died.

Thousands died before they reached the land of refuge. Relatives, afraid to take time to bury or cremate the dead, had to leave bodies to vultures and dogs. Sometimes Hindus were able to drop a hot coal in the mouths of their dead or singe the body in lieu of cremation.

The first hundreds had trickled across on March 26, the day after Tikka Khan unleashed his bulldogs on the unsuspecting Bengalis. The next day the stream was a torrent. By April 30, one and a third million had crossed. By September's end nine million were languishing in 950 camps (one and a half million were children under eight), and they were still coming. Imprisoned Sheik Mujib's aging parents were among them.

They were safe from marauding soldiers, but the horror of days past still haunted them. A twelve-year-old girl screamed night after night, "Don't kill my father!" Women kept seeing the mutilated bodies of young girls, hanging naked from trees, severed breasts piled below—a warning to others who should resist rape. One group told of Pak soldiers luring the young men of their village into giving blood, then draining their bodies until they died. Another group recalled hiding in a jute field near the border when they heard an army patrol approaching. Suddenly an infant in its mother's lap began crying. Unable to quiet the child and fearful of attack, the woman choked her baby to death.

Tikka Khan lured a few back in midsummer by a promise of amnesty. They found their homes looted or in ashes, crops destroyed. Soldiers "welcomed" them with guns; Bihari collaborators robbed some at knifepoint. One hopeful father and his two teen-age daughters were stopped by military as they neared their home village. While the father watched in helpless torment, the soldiers chain-raped the girls. When the soldiers' lusts were slaked the three turned back toward India, the only refuge they knew.

Itself one of the world's poorest nations, India opened its heart to all who came. School terms were cut short to provide shelter in classrooms. Tents and tarpaulins were thrown up to ward off the daily rains that came during the monsoons. Precious food and medicines were shared. The allotment was only fifteen cents per person each day, but even this was a sacrifice for the Indian government.

Many Indian Christians living along the long border literally gave the shirts and saris off their backs. The Indian state of Assam fed and clothed thousands of Christian Garos fleeing from northwestern East Pakistan. "They gave more than

I ever thought possible," reported the Reverend Rochunga Pudaite, the Hmars spiritual leader.

It was inevitable that India should seek U.N. aid. U Thant launched the first worldwide appeal on May 19. U.N. agencies, the Red Cross, CARE, Britain's OXFAM, the world churches began responding.

Catholic agencies of many nations plugged into Caritas India, which was already in operation with eighty-five full-time diocesan directors. The Catholic Medical Mission Board of New York sent thirty-seven and one half tons of medicines on a single airlift.

Supplied by Catholic agencies abroad, Caritas India serviced seventy-one camps in a highly efficient fashion. Field workers in each camp received a list of critical needs daily from the camp director. These were immediately passed on to a diocesan director who had a pipeline to many charitable groups. A typical week brought orders for soap, disinfectants, medicines, tarpaulins, tents, mats, bleaching powder, blankets, clothing, field telephones, sewing machines, maternity kits, syringes, vitamins, and public address systems.

They served in the spirit of the prayer framed on the wall of Mother Teresa's convent in Calcutta: "Make us worthy, Lord, to serve our fellow men who live and die in poverty and hunger. Give them through our hands this day their daily bread. . . ."

Foreign Protestant agencies serviced some camps in cooperation with Indian counterparts and worked with Catholic and secular groups in others. Church World Service, for example, pumped aid to the Christian Agency for Social Action, Relief and Development (CASA), the relief arm of the National Christian Council of India. The World Council of Churches, Lutheran World Relief, and the East Asia Christian Conference also helped CASA. Thus aided, CASA fielded twenty-eight medical teams, operated eight field hospitals, and fed a hundred thousand mothers and babies.

The evangelical U.S. World Relief Commission and The Evangelical Alliance Relief Fund (TEAR) of Britain backed the Evangelical Fellowship of India. The Mennonite Central Committee, Salvation Army, Medical Assistance Programs (MAP), World Vision, and other agencies representing conservative Protestants abroad gave extensive help. One refugee camp was operated by a Hindu mission.

Some of the American organizations obtained huge stocks of surplus food from their government. MAP and the Catholic Medical Mission Board solicited hundreds of tons of medicines from U.S. pharmaceutical companies.

As the year dragged on and the flow of refugees continued, it became apparent that mammoth support had to be solicited and sustained. This necessitated an incessant flow of on-the-scene reports and photographs back from the camps. Such gripping narratives as these loosened the purse strings of millions in the United States and Europe:

> When I started to get in the jeep, I couldn't lift my legs. I looked down and saw a woman wrapped around my legs. She wouldn't let go. I turned to my American missionary friend and asked, "What do I do now?" He said, "I don't know. I've got the same problem." It was very difficult getting them to turn loose. The woman on my legs had just arrived, having traveled two weeks with no food but grass and leaves and now having nothing to feed her children. The other woman was equally hungry. We pointed them to the registration tent where they would be enrolled to receive a cup of food per person each day.
>
> We drove to a crowded medical tent. Just as we were going in a man beside me collapsed in an advanced state of cholera. A doctor put him on saline immediately and told us, "In the

last 24 hours we've lost five from cholera." He waved his arms to scatter the flies from patients.

When we came out into the fresh air, two women held up little emaciated babies. "There is nothing we can do," the missionary said sadly. "You must get in the line for the medical tent." They burst into tears. I looked and saw why. The line stretched as far as the eye could see.

But the most appalling sight I saw was a terminal ward of cholera and typhoid patients in a field hospital. I noticed the ward was open along the sides, letting the monsoon rains blow in on the dying patients. "We had thick plastic sheets there until two nights ago," a doctor said. "Then the Naxalites (a radical Communist group) raided the hospital. They'll use the plastic sheeting to make bombs."

George Hoffman, Director of TEAR,
Britain.

At the camps I saw hundreds of sick, emaciated, dehydrated babies on the edge of death. Too weak to voice a cry they made only dry, rasping sounds. These sounds will live with me forever. . . . The further I went the more shocked I became until I felt engulfed by the seemingly endless acres of agony and death. My sensibilities couldn't absorb any more tragedy. I didn't want to eat, I couldn't sleep. I didn't even want to talk. . . . Before I went there I don't think I ever thanked God when I heard a baby give a lusty cry. Now I do.

I saw food lines everywhere. The lines seemed to be swallowed up by the continuously shifting people who have no place to go. Sometimes the hungry ones have to wait in 110 degree heat or in monsoon rains for as long as eight hours to be served once every three days.

Shelters are made from anything available. They may be little shanties or large construction pipes or an endless row of long bamboo buildings roofed with tarpaulins or polyester sheets.

In these long buildings the family is allotted a space about three by six feet with no privacy. I noticed that many families put up makeshift fences or laid sticks on the ground to define the boundary of their "home."

I saw a child kneeling beside her dying mother, trying to get some response. Two smaller children, not much more than toddlers and naked, played listlessly in refuse nearby. They showed signs of severe malnutrition with bloated tummies and hair turning red from protein deficiency. The child beside the mother, about five, wore a piece of cloth matching her mother's sari. She held up a tiny bony hand begging from the restless throngs. . . . They had troubles enough of their own and no one even glanced at her or her mother.

> *Everett Graffam, Executive Vice President,*
> *World Relief Commission,*
> *United States.*

Father Michael Doheny and I met a little family, a mother, father, and girl of 12. The girl's face was covered with small-pox and she kept her face turned from the sun because she couldn't bear to see the light. The parents were pushing her in a rickshaw which had in it two blankets, a couple of ragged garments, four or five pots and pans and a storm lantern. It was all they had left in the world. We gave them a little money and the mother cried tears of gratitude. A few steps on we turned and looked back, "Who do they remind you of?" I asked my companion.

His eyes were dimmed with tears. "The Holy Family," he said, and I agreed.

> *Father Dermot Doran, Representative of*
> *Catholic Relief Services, United States.*

These and similar reports (printed and given verbally in churches) plus ads in church publications and big-city newspapers drew millions of dollars that helped keep the refugees alive.

Barry Farber, a New York radio personality, saw an ad in the New York *Times* placed by the Catholic Medical Mission Board. A picture showed a child being pulled away from its dead mother and the appeal read: "A mother had died of cholera an hour before, but the infant, less than a year old, continued to nurse until a doctor came upon the scene and pulled him gently away. You can help today."

Farber called Father Joseph Walter, board director, and interviewed him by telephone. One of many responses came from a man in Connecticut who mailed his Christmas cards early. In each of eighty cards he enclosed a check made out to the board for refugee relief and asked the recipient to write a matching check and mail both on to Father Walter. The receipts from the early Christmas mailing totaled $700.

After George Hoffman of TEAR spoke at Oxford, students in the Christian Union fasted with sponsors paying each participant so much for each hour of going without food. They raised £800. Hoffman sent the money to Ben Wati, director of the Evangelical Fellowship of India. The Indian church leader wrote back, "This is the third sponsored fast gift we had. One came from a colony of lepers."

Many church youth groups sponsored "hunger marches," with sponsors contributing so much for each man-mile walked. The "Walking Champion" for the Bengali refugees was Mark Sharman, a twenty-two-year-old former Communist and graduate student at Reading University in England. He raised $24,000 for TEAR by walking from Westminister Abbey in London to Jerusalem.

But the massive relief program was only keeping the refugees alive. The Indian government and world humanitarians could not go on feeding and clothing them forever. The

Indian schools used for housing had to be reopened. Indian peasants living near the camps were complaining that the refugees were faring better than they.

By the end of October the number of refugees had climbed to ten million—more than the population of many nations.

There had to be a political solution.

The Catholic Archbishop of Calcutta, near the largest camps, scolded the world in a public statement.

> The nations of the world have repeatedly refused to intervene in the frightful sufferings of the population of East Bengal. They have washed their hands of the affair on the grounds that "it is purely an internal matter." This severe and uncharitable attitude has surprised and pained us here. When we see millions of men reduced to nothing, made homeless and forced to seek refuge in sordid camps, we declare that their well-being should be concern for all nations. . . . Here more than 70 million . . . have been crushed by the armed forces of their own nation for the simple reason that they won a clear victory in a free election.

The archbishop of Paris, Francis Cardinal Marty, speaking for the French Catholic hierarchy, agreed.

> The first task is to help the millions of refugees. But we should not be content with material aid. Political solutions are called for, and these are the concern of the individual governments. They should do all in their power to restore the conditions necessary for the return of the refugees. We find it hard, therefore, to accept the fact that the arms sold by different nations, including France, should possibly contribute to the violent repression in Pakistan.

U.S. voices for the Bengali cause were few. Norman Cousins in the *Saturday Review* early condemned the Pak government for genocide. He termed the events in Pakistan "a test of American compassion and conscience."* Senator Edward Kennedy, chairman of the Senate Sub-Committee on Refugees, made a "fact-finding" trip through the camps in August (he was refused permission to visit East Pakistan). He called for the United States to stop giving arms and economic assistance to West Pakistan and said there could be "no final solution" to the crisis until West Pakistan made a "political accommodation" with East Pakistan. Senator Eugene McCarthy advocated outright independence for the Bengalis.

American church journals gave wide coverage to reports smuggled out by missionaries inside East Pakistan. The liberal *Christian Century* spoke of the need for political solutions. The United Church of Christ passed a resolution deploring "the flouting of the democratic process in Pakistan," and called on President Nixon and Congress to "suspend general economic aid." Conservative Protestant groups, who supported practically all the American non-Catholic missionaries in East Pakistan, were generally silent on the political issues.

Yahya Khan had not changed his line. He still insisted in October that the rebellion was quashed and the refugees could come home. He was willing to permit a few U.N. relief workers inside the Bengali province, but disdained offers of aid, saying in effect, "Thank you, but we can take care of our own people."

His credibility gap was too wide for even the most gullible to believe.

*May 22, 1971, p. 21.

VII

How Long, O Lord, How Long?

THEY HAD notified both the Indian and Pakistani governments exactly when and where their relief truck would cross
the border and even handed out press announcements. Indian officials made no objections. And Ellen Connett, the
trim, auburn-haired, idealistic American who had met her
husband Paul while publicizing suffering in Biafra could not
believe the Paks would refuse to let the truck pass.

She was wrong.

They sent a second and a third truck. The Paks remained
adamant.

They stopped the notifications and publicity and a few
trucks got across. Then the Paks deported a team of relief
workers and tightened border security.

Operation Omega was stymied. Or was it?

The Connetts and their co-conspirators in mercy held to
the optimistic beliefs of Catholic theologian Teilhard de
Chardin, who taught that mankind was steadily moving to-
wards the "Omega Point" of oneness in love and goodness.
The Pak border guards seemed to be exceptions.

After the trucks were stopped, Paul Connett and a Bengali doctor slipped across with medicines and picked up a Mukti Bahini escort. Two days later Ellen heard about the possibility of reaching the Catholic mission at Simulia near Jessore. She wrote Paul a note and left with a young Englishman named Gordon Slaven on a mission of mercy.

The nine hours of boat travel was exhausting, but still the trip seemed a breeze when they pulled up to shore at the mission station. They were not worried, for they had been told the station was in Mukti territory.

The priests welcomed them joyfully and gave them comfortable rooms for rest. But the next morning they were awakened by Pak soldiers and arrested for crossing the border illegally. On October 11 a hastily convened court sentenced them both to a Jessore prison.

Paul Connett got back to India safely and found his wife's note. He waited for her return. Then, convinced that she and young Slaven had been caught, he flew to Washington in hopes of getting the State Department to obtain her release.

While the two Omegans languished in separate sections of the Jessore prison the monsoons dripped to an end. With better arms from sympathetic Indian border-security guards, the Muktis began moving out of their camps, mostly along the Indian border, for bolder forays.

In mid-October the Mukti began drawing Pak troops into open battles. By November they controlled sizable hunks of territory along the border and were operating gunboats in the Bay of Bengal. Their strength was now estimated at twenty to twenty-five thousand against about ninety thousand government soldiers.

World tensions were rising over sharpening Asian political alignments around what seemed to be an inevitable Indo-Pakistan war. The August Indo-Soviet "friendship" treaty had excited China, an ally of Pakistan. There were rumors that the Soviets had promised to replace all arms that India wished to give the Muktis. Pro-Soviet and pro-Chinese Communist elements were said to be maneuvering for influence within the Bengali resistance movement. The U.N. talked but would not act. The Nixon administration stood pat on professed neutrality and noninterference in Pakistan's affairs. The Muktis and India felt the administration's sympathies still lay with Pakistan. Nervous nellies on the diplomatic circuit feared the festering Bengali problem could flare into World War III with Pakistan and China marshalled against India and the Soviet Union.

As worried world-watchers waited nervously and diplomats conferred, the foreign missionaries inside East Pakistan kept open their channels of compassion. An Islamic scholar in Dacca who observed their commitment told a CORR worker, "Only the Christians are living up to the teachings of the Holy Koran in this present crisis."

Only the missionaries could travel with reasonable safety across both Pak and Mukti territories. Though two foreign priests had been killed, they still felt the government did not want to incite condemnation from the Pope or other world church leaders.

Phil Parshall traveled for three days in a small rowboat through a web of small canals to a Mukti hospital. He talked to a wounded guerilla amputee. "I'm ready to go and fight again for my country," the young Bengali said. The Muktis took Phil to nine starving Hindu families who were despairing of life. He gave $20 to each family.

Still there was danger in travel. There were checkpoints at almost every street corner and crossroads. Though they drove at night with their dome lights on, there was always the possibility of driving past a checkpoint by mistake. For

Bengali churchmen, unescorted by foreigners, the danger was greater. "It was push, kick, slap at every stop for me," observed round-faced Matthew Malakar, the treasurer of the Bengali Protestant Council of Churches. "But when a missionary was along they acted like gentlemen."

Mines and bombs were other hazards. Sister Emanuel, a French nun, died when her jeep struck a mine near Mymensingh. Goot Gustafson, a red-haired Swedish Pentecostal, saw a bomb explode only two hundred yards away in downtown Dacca killing ten and destroying seven cars. The Assemblies of God's Josephine Spina, who had returned from the first evacuations, missed a blast by only two minutes in the American Express office in Chittagong. One day Cal Olson went home instead of to a government office in Dacca as planned. A bomb went off in that building at the time he would have been there. Others had similar experiences.

Throughout November the missionaries continued to risk their lives in aiding hungry and sick people whom the government ignored at best and oppressed at worst.

A British Baptist missionary, who must go unnamed, was dubbed "Rear Admiral" by his colleagues. He ran a fleet of eleven relief boats in the maze of waterways around Barisal. His boats were stopped by both Muktis and soldiers and searched for arms. During one interception Muktis fed him and his boatmen a good dinner, then showed off their store of old World War II weapons along with modern Indian automatics and grenades. When a Mukti started to demonstrate a grenade, the "Admiral" held up a hand and said he had seen enough.

Leaving his family at the crowded Southern Baptist mission house in Dacca, Jim McKinley took money given by Australian and New Zealand Baptists and hired workers to build two hundred low-cost houses in villages that still hadn't recovered from the cyclone. Tom and Gloria Thurman took their children back to Faridpur and reopened the Christian Industrial Center. Gloria wrote to assure their families back in Mississippi and Alabama:

> In all that has happened, God has been so very real. He has protected us from harm and given His precious peace in troubled days. He has taught a clearer meaning of bearing the burdens of one another. We believe that after great suffering, God is able to do great things. We are praying that we shall see this here.
>
> The people continue to come and we continue to listen. If they find something of God's love, then our staying will not be in vain.

Their reasons for staying were shared by other missionaries who kept telling the Bengalis that God was on the side of justice, that the long night of fear and oppression would soon be ending. But this was hard for a father whose daughters had been stolen, or a mother who had seen her son shot before her eyes to understand.

Cal and Marian Olson in Dacca were not unlike others who went to bed emotionally drained every night. On Friday evening, November 5, after a long day of consoling and counseling, Cal was roused by three West Pakistani strangers asking for literature. He gave them some Gospels and tracts and they left.

Two of them returned the next evening with the same request. As he bent to get some materials off a shelf, the inquirers pulled daggers and told Cal not to move. At the same moment a masked man burst through the door waving a gun and ordered, "Get in a corner!"

Believing they planned to kill him, the skinny Assembly of God missionary refused. Suddenly his wife opened the door and asked what was going on. One of the men rushed toward her with a dagger and she screamed.

"Don't harm her!" Olson shouted. "Come upstairs. You can have everything."

From the Olsons' apartment the robbers took relief money, church offerings, and Cal's wedding ring. Then after tying and gagging the couple with strips ripped from Cal's *lunghi,* they left. Frightened servants who had been hiding outside rushed in and untied them.

David Roland, a British Baptist, was tied up and beaten by Pak soldiers for a different reason. They charged him with being a spy for India.

Roland's colleague, David Stockley, was picked up near the British Baptist Hospital at Chondragona, and accused of spying for the Mukti Bahinis. When he asked them to be more specific, an officer snarled, "You have been working against the best interests of Pakistan."

Stockley, a heavy man with bright ginger-red hair, blew up. An agriculturist, he had introduced miracle rice and other crops to thousands of impoverished farmers.

"I—I," he fumed. "You are the ones. You have interfered with my work by destroying crops and seeds needed by hungry people." He continued his lecture until the officer snapped in disgust, "Let him go."

But Holy Cross Father William Evans did not get off so lightly. Saturday afternoon, November 13, the fifty-two-year-old U.S. citizen was in a small boat headed for Boxonogore, a rural mission station, to say mass. Soldiers who motioned him to the bank could see that he was wearing a cassock.

He asked his boatman to comply. The soldiers ordered him to report to the nearby military camp. After a few minutes, he came out accompanied by five Pakistan soldiers. He was about to step back into his boat when the officer in charge

ordered him to sit in a ditch. They knocked him down with
their rifles, slashed him with their bayonets, then shot him
twice and booted his body into the river. The body was
recovered by local people and secretly brought back to Golla,
his home station, for burial.

Archbishop Ganguly came from Dacca to view the body
and hear the terrified boatman's eyewitness account. Father
Evans was perhaps the best-loved priest in the country and
known for his gentleness and soft speaking. Five thousand
sorrowing Muslims, Hindus, and Christians attended his fu-
neral.

The crusty Father Goedert at Nagari was shattered when
he heard the news. "Bill Evans came over on the same boat
with me," he told the missionary messenger. "He was the last
man among us who would have provoked a shooting. I can
see them coming after me—but Bill? It was cold deliberate
murder."

Father Goedert had no time for extended grief. He wrote
CORR:

> We watch the fires of burning villages in hopeless despera-
> tion. There is nothing we can do; there is no authority we can
> appeal to.
>
> Each day is worse than the previous one. For two days we
> had to turn hungry people away. When we finally got in a
> boatload of flour and began the distribution, one old woman
> couldn't wait. As she was walking away with her flour, she
> stuffed a handful of the stuff into her mouth. Try it sometime.
> You've got to be hungry.

And a few days later:

> It has finally happened. I have lost my credit rating in the
> local business community. Up till now, I was considered a
> good risk. I would be owing thousands of rupees to the local

merchants for the food they were bringing in. They felt their money was safer with me, and would come around to collect it when they were ready to buy again. As of two days ago I have to pay cash on delivery. It has nothing to do with my honesty or solvency. They have lost faith in my ability to survive.

By the end of November fighting between the Mukti rebels and the Pak army was approaching full-scale warfare. Border incidents with Indian soldiers were occurring regularly. Both India and Pakistan beefed up troop strength along their western borders in anticipation that fighting would soon start in disputed Kashmir.

Pak atrocities among the Bengalis seemed to be rising to the level of the previous April. More villages were burned. More civilians were killed.

And still the army seemed to show a curious ambivalence toward Bengali Christians. Reports to missionaries indicated Christians were being spared in some places, killed in others.

Banjit Dhali, the caretaker at the Adventist church in Dingadahl, near Dacca, was taken out three times to be shot. The first two times the soldiers decided he was needed to cut wood and haul water while they were mining the property. Having planted the explosives, they called him before a firing squad for the third time. When they raised their rifles he fell to his knees and began praying audibly. One member of the squad broke ranks, saying, "I am a Christian. I can't shoot him." He walked over and kicked the caretaker, then in a scolding way told him to run for his life. He did and survived.

Sudhir Adhikari, a prominent Baptist layman, had a harrowing experience in his home village. His brother was preaching when soldiers and local Bihari informers poured into the church. The soldiers ordered the teen-agers outside where they made them do monkey tricks such as putting thumbs in ears and squatting up and down.

They let the teens return to their parents and asked the Biharis to identify Hindus in the congregation. Four were pointed out and they were taken outside and executed. A few minutes later an officer drove up. He asked questions, learned what had happened, and apologized to the people.

But no apologies were made for the murder of Christians in many villages. For example, Matthew Malakar received word that troops had entered his home village near Barisal and charged seven Christians with aiding the Mukti Bahini. They were taken to the marketplace and shot in full view of a crowd. The same happened to five Christians in the neighboring village of Muladi.

Nor were Christians spared in the last days of November around Nagari. The worst massacre came on the Sunday evening after Thanksgiving when soldiers raced through nearby Ranga Matti village, throwing torches into flimsy, dry bamboo huts. They shot fleeing villagers, mostly women and children. Those unable to escape were lined up and executed in the light of the fires. Sixteen Christians were among the victims.

Five days later Pak planes swept across the rice paddies. The refugees in Father Goedert's school scattered into the jungle as the planes dropped bombs barely a mile away.

Father Goedert jammed a change of clothing into a flight bag and raced out the back door. He almost tripped over four old women on the porch. "Run for your lives!" he shouted. "The planes will be bombing here any minute."

A wrinkled face looked up at him in quiet resignation. "We're too old to run, Father. We'll stay and die with you."

He put down his flight bag and invited the women inside.

VIII

Joi Bangla!

THE ABWEY missionaries at Malumghat Hospital in the far south enjoyed a happy but apprehensive Thanksgiving. Their older children were safely home for winter vacation from mission high school in Murree, West Pakistan. They had obtained the last seats on one of the last commercial flights to Dacca. Upon arriving home, seventeen-year-old Tom Ketcham had promptly gone hunting in the adjoining jungle and killed a two-hundred-pound wild boar.

The Pak army had continued to follow their April decision not to bother villages in the zone where hospital employees lived. No bullets had sliced across the twenty-five acres of leased hospital property. But the evidences of war elsewhere were ample: refugees pleading for food and medicine, Hindus begging for conversion, and tragic gunshot victims being brought in daily. Dr. Ketcham had removed the eye of a five-year-old girl and repaired the shattered bowel of a boy the same age. Both had been shot by Pak troops outside the "neutral" zone.

The times were trying for the missionary mothers at the

hospital as they nervously watched their children playing "war." Posing as a Pak soldier, eleven-year-old Marty Ketcham would point his wooden gun at a playmate and yell, "I'm a Punjabi. What are you?" If the answer was, "Bengali," the boy would shout, "Bang! Bang! You're dead." Then they might switch roles with the "Bengali" shooting the "Punjabi" and yelling *"Joi Bangla!"* The mothers worried that a child would shout the wrong slogan before the wrong visitor.

At the turn of the month there was a pickup in gunshot patients. Some whispered to the doctors that the climactic battles were coming, that independence for Bangladesh would come soon. Dr. Paul Adolph, a recently arrived short-termer and missionary in China before the Communist take-over, remarked grimly, "Just like old times."

India's Prime Minister Indira Gandhi returned from a three-week tour of western nations with only a few pledges for Bengali refugee relief. She reportedly had told President Nixon that her country sympathized with the Bengali inde-pendence movement, but had no intention of going to war.

Her hawkish Parliament was chafing at the bit for direct action against Pakistan. The refugee cost to India (560 mil-lion people with only a $50 billion gross national product) was running a million dollars a day. Legislators claimed that 2,800 Pak regulars had recently crossed the border. A bloody frontier battle had just been fought. Still Mrs. Gandhi asked for patience in the hope that western leaders would pressure Yahya Khan into a political solution agreeable to the Ben-galis.

Yahya Khan was intransigent. "If she [Mrs. Gandhi] wants war," he snapped, "I'll give it to her." As he spoke both sides were probing and harassing the other with artillery and snip-ing along the borders.

The cards were obviously stacked in favor of India. The

world's second largest nation outnumbered both East and West Pakistan in population almost four to one. India's troop strength, east and west, more than doubled that of Pakistan's. Around the 1,300-mile border of East Pakistan 200,000 Indian troops almost completely encircled the Bengali province. With the Muktis and their millions of supporters inside, the Pak Army faced enemies from every direction. And supplies and reinforcements from the west could only be brought in by sea or air.

World governments pleaded for restraint, but the fuse had been allowed to burn too close.

At 5:45 P.M., December 3, the Pak air force launched preemptive air strikes against seven Indian airfields. The Indians had taken precautions and lost not one plane.

Near or about the same time, Indian troops began moving on a large scale.

Exactly which was the aggressor may never be known. The Soviets blamed Pakistan. The United States and China accused India of striking first. The White House charged that Mrs. Gandhi's trip to Washington had been a smokescreen for massive war preparations by her generals.

Regardless, war between the two populous nations raged in East Pakistan and along the border in the west.

The Indians quickly took the initiative. Within two days of the Pak air strikes, the Indian air force wiped out Pak planes in the east. The Indians then quickly blockaded Chittagong and Chalna harbors, cutting the last link between East and West Pakistan. On the ground Indian infantry and artillery pushed deep into the Bengali province.

U.S. efforts for disengagement by both sides were blocked by Soviet *nyets* in the U.N. Security Council. By the time the wrangling General Assembly could agree on a demand for a ceasefire and withdrawal, Indian victory was certain. While the Indian government stalled on the diplomatic front, its forces continued rapid advances.

The high commands of both countries had studied war strategy together in British war colleges. The Paks expected the Indians to pursue traditional tactics: thrust forward and capture a strongpoint, regroup and take on reinforcements, then move on to the next objective. But India's commander on the eastern front, Lieutenant-General J. S. Aurora, launched a lightning, zigzag strategy to capture some cities, while bypassing others and reach Dacca in twelve to fifteen days. Dacca was surrounded by a moat of rivers and marshes. Given enough time, he feared the Paks might turn the capital into an island fortress.

Jessore, straight across the border from Calcutta, was the first major city to fall. During her two months' imprisonment, Omegan Ellen Connett, who had discovered she was pregnant, had frequently heard the sound of gunfire. She heard firing and bombing closer when Indian planes bombed the Pak army headquarters and the Jessore airport. But neither she nor her barrack mates—twenty Bengali women and five young children—could see over the twelve-foot walls. Except for the guards who brought their skimpy vegetable meals three times a day, they had seen no one from outside. Acutely aware of her pregnancy, Ellen hoped fervently for deliverance.

On the morning of December seventh the gunfire was louder, almost as if a battle was going on across the street. The prison children huddled to their mothers, whimpering softly. There was a sudden silence, then from outside the high wall came shouts of *"Joi Bangla! Joi Bangla!"*

Ellen had never heard the words before. But the prisoners had. From the prison complex six hundred voices roared back, *"Joi Bangla! Joi Bangla!"*

At 8 P.M. the prison doors were flung open by Mukti Bahini. In the confusion Ellen managed to find her young English friend, Gordon Slaven. He was thin and weak, but otherwise in good health. Later in the evening a smiling Indian general came and made arrangements for them to fly to Calcutta. The priest at the Simulia mission had told him two foreigners were in the prison.

In Calcutta Ellen learned that Paul was still in Washington working with the State Department to negotiate for her release. She flew to join him for a joyful Christmas.

At Nagari, on the eastern side of the Ganges River, Father Goedert and his four old women had survived the Pakistani air attack of late November. The refugees had returned again from their jungle hideaways. Now they scattered once more upon hearing gunfire from the east. Father Goedert sighed and made the old women comfortable. Then he bedded down on a floor mattress. He wondered if this might not be the end for all of them.

Toward morning he heard explosions coming from the south. He looked toward the Dacca airport and saw planes diving and bombing. He knew for the first time that India had entered the war.

Later in the day Indian troops came marching along the railroad track, headed for Dacca. With no transportation possible in the area, the liberators had to carry all their equipment by hand.

When news spread around that the troops were from India, refugees began pouring down the levee, waving flags and flowers in joyful greeting. Women carried bushel baskets of precious *chapattis* bread to feed them. The men and boys begged to help carry guns, shells, and other equipment.

The gaunt priest, who was down to 145 pounds, was not one to show emotion. But this day was an exception. He grabbed a flag and shouted *Joi Bangla* with the rest.

Further north at the Church of God hospital in Bogra, Dr. Eva Gilbert and her staff were caught between battling Indian and Pak troops. For two days they lay in a ditch and prayed while artillery whistled overhead. When the Paks finally retreated, a smiling Indian colonel came to check on their safety.

When he heard of their ordeal, he exclaimed, "What courage!"

Dr. Gilbert smiled back. "Faith, not courage. Come in and have some tea."

In the far southeast, the Howard Hawkes at the Assemblies of God main station at Khulna heard the Indian artillery as they were sitting down to eat. "We'd better get in the trench back of the house," Hawkes told his wife. Leaving their food on the table, they ran to the trench. Minutes later, a shell slammed through the kitchen wall, showering the table with glass. They stayed in the trench until the Indian troops had swept past.

Dacca was a city under siege as Indian planes strafed and bombed the airport and military encampment. General A. A. Niazi stubbornly refused "invitations" to surrender, vowing he would see the city reduced to rubble first.

Not knowing that full-scale war would start, Cal Olson had planned an evangelistic crusade. An Arab preacher flew in the day before the Indians began bombing the airport. When the bombs began falling, Cal said, "This can't be much worse than what we've already lived through. Let's go ahead. We'll have services at 3:30 in the afternoon so people can get home before the curfew."

Neighbors and refugees staying with the Olsons made the attendance better than in peacetime. The singing, praying, and preaching blended in with pounding of bombs and pow-

pow of anti-aircraft fire. Many Bengalis became Christians.

After a day or so it became clear that the Indians were bombing only military targets and were good marksmen at that. The missionaries went on with their business, drawing in only at night when a shoot-to-kill curfew was enforced.

One morning Cal Olson visited a wounded college professor in a hospital. "I've lost faith in my Muslim religion," the intellectual said. "Do you have a book that tells the truth about God?" Olson gave him Billy Graham's *Peace with God*.

The Catholic missionaries in Dacca kept CORR operating. Father Charles Young from upstate New York was one of the boldest. His face deeply lined from almost forty years under the Asian sun, Father Young bribed his way through roadblocks and carried food to refugees in two Catholic missions. One afternoon near the airport the bombs were falling too close for comfort. He halted his jeep and ducked into a building at Holy Cross College. "Just in time for tea, Father" a smiling nun said as she directed him to the sisters' "shelter" under stairs. When he marveled at their calmness, his hostess replied, "This is the eighteenth time in twenty-four hours we've come in here. So we're used to it."

The pressure was on all foreigners in the capital. Most huddled in the Intercontinental Hotel, declared a "neutral" haven by the International Red Cross. They were offered the chance to evacuate on Sunday morning, December twelfth, when both combatants were pledged to stay clear of the airport area.

The U.S. consulate recommended that the missionaries also be on the planes.

The three Southern Baptist families were back together again. They discussed the consulate's recommendation under a table while a Pak anti-aircraft battery across the street blasted away at Indian planes. Their decision was to stay. Dr.

John Freeman, a visiting Southern Baptist missionary medic from Thailand who had flown in a day before the bombing began felt he might be needed more in Dacca.

The remaining missionaries, Protestant and Catholic, made the same decision. Sunday morning they saw the U.N. planes circle in, then take off with their loads. Even Mark Tucker, the Texas deacon from the Cholera lab, was going.

One of the Bengalis sheltered by the Olsons saw the planes and asked Cal, "Why didn't you go?"

"We believe God wants us here with our friends" the slim Minnesotan replied.

The Bengali rolled his eyes in incomprehension and said, "Well I would have gone if I could!"

The Parshalls (one child) and the Stuart Averys (four children) from New Zealand tried to explain to their children why they weren't on the planes. "We feel God will take care of us here," Phil said. "He won't let the bombs hit us."

There were now left in Dacca about fifteen evangelical missionaries plus dependents, over a hundred foreign Catholic priests, brothers, and nuns (mostly from the United States), skeleton staffs of the foreign consulates, thirty-four U.N. personnel, and fifteen to twenty foreign journalists.

Indian troops were moving fast on the capital.

Then came foreign radio reports that the U.S. nuclear-powered carrier *Enterprise* and a flotilla of supporting ships from the Seventh Fleet had sailed into the Bay of Bengal. The U.S. Navy said the armada was there to rescue American civilians, principally missionaries, if necessary. The Bengali "freedom radio" disagreed, saying the American ships planned to intervene and rescue Pakistani troops. The announcement that Soviet vessels were moving toward the area suggested that a big-power confrontation was in the offing. A third report hinted that the American ships were there to ward off a Soviet-Chinese clash. Whatever the reason, the Bengalis saw the ships as a threat against their fight for independence.

But Pak forces were in control of Dacca and they did not feel kindly toward the Soviets, who had backed their enemy. So great was the fear of the Soviet diplomats that on the night of the fifteenth they fled to the American consulate, crying "God save us all! Pray for us." The American who let them in was not sympathetic. "You SOB's don't even believe in God," he reportedly said. "How can you expect Him to save you?"

Shortly after dawn the Indian lead column linked up with paratroopers flown in from Calcutta on the outskirts of the city. General Gandharv Nagra, the column commander, sent an odd surrender request to Pak General Niazi. "My dear Abdullah, I am here. The game is up. I suggest you give yourself up to me and I'll look after you." The explanation was that the two had been friends some years before when General Nagra had served with the Indian High Commission in West Pakistan.

Actually Niazi had wanted to surrender two days before, but could not obtain authorization from Yahya Khan in West Pakistan. This time the military president surfaced and radioed his okay.

When the Instrument of Surrender was signed at 4:31 P.M. on the Dacca Race Course a mammoth Bengali crowd went wild with joy. Cheering young men hoisted turbaned General Aurora, the Indian Commander-in-Chief, to their shoulders. Others kissed Indian soldiers, pushed marigolds up their gun barrels and garlanded their caps with jasmine. In exploding ecstasy thousands of Bengalis waved flags and pictures of their beloved Sheik Mujib and roared *"Joi Bangla! Joi Bangla!"* in thunderous shouts.

The Indians feared that the Bengalis' joy would quickly melt in a passion for revenge. In a rare gesture for a victorious army they permitted Pak troops in Dacca to keep their arms until reaching prison camps.

Pak hold-out forces in other cities began surrendering to the Indians. In Chittagong, missionary Josephine Spina, who had returned soon after the April evacuation, led a thanksgiving service in the Assemblies of God church. Her British Baptist neighbors on the hill, who had never left, shared in the service.

Across town three single Abweys were glad the war was over. Reid Minich had never left during the terrible nine months. Ernajean Lockerbie and Lynn Silvernail had returned with their colleagues in late May and sheltered a house full of Bengali girls the rest of the time.

The Abweys at Malumghat Hospital had also remained at their posts. The last ship into Chittagong before the Indian blockade closed the port had brought two tons of medicines for the hospital from Medical Assistance Programs. The next day a roving band of Muktis mistook Abwey Melvin Beals for a Punjabi on the road to Chittagong. When they brought him to a guerilla camp, he convinced their leader that he was from the hospital. The Mukti officer begged his pardon and gave him his bed for the night.

A week later a contingent of Muktis swarmed into the hospital compound and demanded that the missionaries fly the Bangladesh flag. They altered an old Pakistani flag and raised it. Kitty Ketcham began making a new flag.

The following day an Indian plane circled low overhead. The children climbed onto the Ketcham's roof and watched the plane drop bombs on a reputed hideout for Pak collaborators about a half mile away. No one was in the building.

The Muktis returned with a political delegation for an offi-

cial ceremony. The ragged but proud Bengalis, dark eyes
gleaming, stood barefoot at attention as Kitty Ketcham's new
flag was lifted in front of the hospital. When it reached the
top of the pole, the Bengalis stamped the ground, saluted
smartly, and shouted *"Joi Bangla!"*

"Joi Bangla!" the Abweys shouted back. Then Dr.
Ketcham offered a prayer for lasting peace.

Three Indian fliers called at the hospital. "I'm the chap
who circled your place and dropped the bombs across the
road. I tried to signal you to stay away." Then he added. "I'm
a Christian, too."

Someone brought tea and cookies and as the Indian pilots
sipped unhesitantly, Donn Ketcham thought of a Pak general
who had refused to touch their tea until sampled by someone. "They trust us," he whispered to the nurse beside him.

From the tip of Bengali land that wriggled into Burma to
the top that reared into northern India, there was celebra-
tion. Though recognized only by India, Bangladesh, the
world's eighth largest nation in population and second largest Muslim country (Indonesia is first) had become a reality.

The missionaries rejoiced with the excited exuberant Bengalis. Phil Parshall described the birth process of the world's
139th nation as, "a nine-month, full-term waiting period
which included fourteen days of agonizing labor followed by
the bloody caesarean birth."

He added a plea for understanding: "A baby doesn't walk,
much less learn to run overnight. Maturity takes time. Development of the infant requires patience and assistance. Let
the world be not hasty in condemning the faults of the newborn. As Christians, let us feed the hungry, let us bind up the
bleeding, let us give sympathy to the broken-hearted."

The birth did not immediately stop the killing. On the day
of the surrender small groups of Pak soldiers changed to

civilian clothes and ran through Dacca shooting at celebrators at random. But the loose Punjabis were quickly rounded up and hustled off to prison camps where the Indians stood guard against revengeful Bengalis.

Bengali bitterness rose with every new revelation of Pak atrocities. Most arousing was the news that 125 of Dacca's leading intellectuals had been kidnaped and executed by a fanatical Muslim sect of traitorous Biharis and Bengalis only hours before Indian troops had entered the city. Members of the returning government-in-exile showed foreign newsmen their mutilated bodies in a mass grave.

The liberated city broiled in a collective rage. At a public demonstration for the release of Sheik Mujib, still held in West Pakistan, Muktis displayed four trussed-up men whom they said had assaulted Bengali women. Then the Muktis stomped and bayoneted their prisoners to death while the frenzied crowd cheered and newsmen popped pictures.

Tikka Khan, Yahya Khan, and other hated symbols of oppression were out of reach. But Yahya in West Pakistan felt the heat. The stubborn military president resigned in favor of Ali Bhutto, his pro-Chinese deputy prime minister. Bhutto promptly lifted the passports of Pakistan's twenty-two richest families and ordered them to repatriate $280 million hidden abroad, much of this profits from Bengali sweat.

Bhutto refused to recognize the dismemberment of Pakistan, but he released Sheik Mujib and shipped him off to London. Mujib quickly held a press conference and described his imprisonment in the condemned cell of a desert jail. Referring to the atrocities in Bangladesh of which he had just heard, he cried, "If Hitler were alive, he would be ashamed."

The Bengalis welcomed their arriving Bangabandhu ("Friend of Bengal") by screaming thousands at Dacca airport. His wife and children were in the welcoming crowd, including a new grandson named Joi for the liberation slogan.

He quickly proclaimed a provisional constitution, put primary powers in his own hands as prime minister, and appointed a cabinet from his own Awami party. He declared Bangladesh independent of Pakistan and said the country would be nonaligned and would rest on four pillars: democracy, nationalism, secularism, and socialism.

He acknowledged tearfully that the country was worse off than he had thought: 3 million dead, 300,000 women raped, and 30 million destitute (including the 10 million refugees returning from India). The national treasury he said was bare, seventy-five percent of the industry wrecked, and transportation and communication crippled.

Publicly he called for forgiveness, but said Bangladesh reserved the right to try some war criminals if the U.N. failed to act. Privately, when asked about forgiving the million and a half minority of Biharis that had mostly sided with the occupation army, he told newsmen, "You must remember I am not a Christian. I am the son of a Muslim." The inference to the Muslim law of retribution—an eye for an eye and a tooth for a tooth—was obvious.

In the days immediately following, the future of the country looked precarious. There were reports of atrocities against Biharis by Bengali vigilante committees. The Adventist missionaries saw a reverse replay of the previous April as Bengali mobs now swept in to loot and burn Bihari houses. Biharis jammed into police stations begging to be jailed for protection from vengeful Bengalis. Others cowered in their homes or fled into jungles.

There were food riots as prices rose. Hungry mobs smashed shop windows. The prime minister called for the

Muktis to turn in their weapons. But not all did.

Pessimists forecast a second revolution, anarchy, calamitous disaster.

Sheik Mujib appealed for patriotism, sacrifice, and hard work in rebuilding the country. In candor he confessed, "Bangladesh was born with nothing but problems. Bangladesh," he said, "needs and wants assistance from abroad. But not at the price of national honor. We prefer to die as a poor nation rather than make our posterity slaves."

As they had to the refugees in India, world Christians opened their hearts. A lettered plaque on CORR Director Andy Koval's desk expressed the sentiments of all: GOD BLESS THIS MESS.

IX

Inasmuch . . .

BAKSHISH! Bakshish! My mudder and fadder are dead."

"Bakshish! Bakshish! My sons and daughters were killed by soldiers."

The beggars, old and young, were suffocating as we battled through the mid-day crowds outside the Dacca air terminal.

Troy Bennett of the Southern Baptists ran interference for us. "If somebody hasn't already told you," he said after we were safely in the carryall, "there are two things you need to know immediately. "You're from America, but Nixon isn't your name. And a little *'Joi Bangla'* now and then doesn't hurt. The Bengalis love and admire us as individual Americans, but they're less than happy with our government's position during the war."

Troy, a thin Dan Dailey with a big smile, honked his way on to Airport Road. The traffic almost defied description. Colorful dragoned and flowered rickshaws closed around us, pedaled by lean sinewy men and boys, *lunghis* flopping above the hot pavement. Others pulled ponderous carts, or drove sweaty, tail-flicking oxen. Creaky, rusty, horn-blaring taxis clattered by, bearing foreign fares to the Intercontinental Hotel straight ahead. Through it all, jaywalkers were darting and weaving to reach the other side of the street.

"You wouldn't believe a city this crowded could be the way it was during the war," Troy said. "It was eerie with the streets deserted."

The buildings flashing by were duller than the rickshaws. Fresh paint was rare on the plastered walls, but so were bullet holes and other scars of war. Every block or so we caught a cross and the scrawl, Christian House. Closer to the hotel we saw a tent-and-rag city spread across vacant blocks. Flocks of bathers dipping and splashing in a slimy pond near defecating cows underscored the poverty. Thousands of such squatters, Troy said, had seeped into Dacca from the country where their homes and crops had been destroyed. They were surviving only on handouts from relief agencies.

Troy dropped us off at the columned Intercontinental. In the lobby canaries were singing beside a sparkling fountain and around the corner a maharajah's buffet feast was spread for guests. After registering, we got in line behind a tall square-jawed, executive-type from Oregon: Jack Adams, executive director of the Holt Adoption Program.

"If this is your first time, have the buffet," he said. "You won't be able to eat it after you've been here awhile."

Jack had been "looking for babies fathered by Pak soldiers. We're arranging international adoption of these babies who would not be accepted in Bengali society," he said.

How many had he found?

"Less than a hundred. We're assuming a substantial number will be popping up soon and are assigning a case worker to the country. You'll hear all sorts of figures on the number of women raped. I would say between one hundred and four hundred thousand. No one will ever know the exact figure."

After lunch we ran into Gandhi-thin Cal Olson in the cool lobby, his thin shoulders wrapped in a sweater. He had dropped by to see Everett Graffam of the World Relief Commission. When we asked Cal about estimates on war atrocities, he smiled enigmatically. "The Bengalis call something that doesn't exist a 'horse's egg.' That, in this situation, would be accurate statistics. I've heard that three million are dead and thirty million destitute. Perhaps so. All I do know is that I've seen enough death and suffering to last a lifetime."

Toni Hagen, the no-nonsense Swiss chief of U.N. Operations was leaving. Dr. Hagen, a professional geologist and veteran U.N. catastrophe troubleshooter, gave a gloomy summation in an unofficial Information Paper titled "Blunt Facts on Relief and Rehabilitation in Bangladesh:"

> All disaster relief operations in the past have no comparison with the magnitude of the task in Bangladesh. The infrastructure in transport and communications is totally wrecked, the industries are not operational due to difficult legal, monetary and financial problems and due to lack of raw materials. . . . Millions of people return from India . . . to find their homes wrecked, their former fertile land lying idle. The Government administration inherited total chaos after the war. Most of the school buildings are wrecked, furniture and teaching aids, science equipment and books are looted or destroyed.
>
> On the positive side is the resilience of the people. . . . However, even the most inventive and most resilient destitute people have no chance to survive if they are not given a minimum standby to start with. In Bangladesh millions of people have to take off from zero. . . . Food would be available in almost any local market, but the destitute persons have, of

course, no purchasing power. And this is indeed the root of the whole problem:

        (a) poverty;
        (b) poverty and
        (c) poverty.

The primary need, he concluded, was not "blankets, baby food or midwifery kits," but to revive the economy. "The Government," he said, "cannot generate the necessary funds as long as the economy and industries are dead."

For 1972, Hagen projected $439 million as the "absolute minimal aid" for food, housing, transportation, schools, and raw materials and implements for agriculture and industries.

At U.N. headquarters we learned that $376.1 million of this amount had been pledged by sixteen countries. Heading the list was impoverished India ($142.7 million) with the United States in second place ($122.6 million), Canada third ($48.75 million), and tiny Sweden fourth ($12 million). Japan was sixth ($10.6 million), Britain seventh ($8.6 million), West Germany eighth ($7.2 million) and the Soviet Union ninth ($6.8 million).

U.S. aid was flowing quietly through the U.N. and private voluntary agencies. Soviet aid was coming directly and was trumpeted almost daily on the front page of newspapers. A complimentary Russian helicopter and crew carried Sheik Mujib to rallies throughout the country where he was always greeted by cheering throngs. A team of Soviet doctors selected thirty wounded Mukti Bahini for three months of medical care in Moscow. "They picked the thirty easiest cases," a missionary medic grumped to us.

The public relations-minded Soviets had also arranged a $45 million trade agreement: cleaning sunken ships from

Chittagong harbor in exchange for raw cotton. The Bangladesh government had hoped the U.N. would do it, but bureaucratic snarls in New York had given the job to the Russians by one day of default.

The usually mild-mannered American missionaries whom we interviewed uniformly bewailed the failure of U.S. foreign policy. "Our government did a first-class job of blundering up the whole subcontinent," one said. "We opened the door to the Russians and then kicked them in. I hang my head in shame over my country's immoral policies."

The Assemblies of God's Cal Olson and Larry Ward, president of Food for the Hungry, recalled an old man's response to their announcement of food gifts: "Thank you very much. You must be Russians."

The pro-Soviet Communist party was highly active. On the eve of the first May Day propagandists plastered major buildings with slogans. High-toned Marxist literature was selling better in the magazine shop at the Intercon than U.S.-published sex- and violence-saturated paperbacks. Zealous colporteurs peddled Marxist books and magazines on trains. Full-page newspaper features lauded the good life in the Soviet Union.

Opinions of long-term missionaries about the threat of a Communist takeover ranged from pessimistic to uncertain. Understandably, most asked not to be quoted by name.

A sampling:

"I'm not predicting the future at all."

"We're definitely moving toward communism. Prices are rising along with general unrest. The Muktis haven't turned in all their grenades and guns. They know where these are hidden."

"Before it was the oppressed against the oppressor. We will come to a time when it will be Bengali against Bengali. The

Communists are trying to create dissatisfaction in every way possible. They'll never be happy until we go through another bloodbath."

"I've been hearing for fifteen years that the Communists are going to take control. I'm still guardedly optimistic. I think the Lord has a thing or two to do here."

"We have more trouble with some of our supporters back in the United States who think the Communists have already taken over than we do with Communists here. The Communists are not in power in Bangladesh, although they have as much freedom as anyone else. This is a democratic country for the first time. There is a spiritual vacuum which can be filled with either communism or Christianity. We've never had such opportunities. Why, the Bible is now read over national radio along with the Koran, Sunday is the day of rest instead of Friday, the Muslim holy day."

"Remember people said Muslim Indonesia would go Communist. Instead, millions have become Christians there. God could do the same here. The Bengalis know what the Christian minority did during the fight for independence. They know what the missions and Christian relief groups are doing now."

We asked Rab Choudhury, the self-possessed government Coordinator of External Relief and Rehabilitation, about the last statement.

Barefooted and with a patriotic gleam in his eyes, he spoke to us from behind a desk stacked high with plans and reports of forty-eight foreign agencies. "I am not a Christian," he said candidly, "but I am not anti-Christian. I tell you we Bengalis feel deep respect for the missionaries who talk more of humanity than of Christianity. They are helping us in ways we can see."

He patted a stack of papers. "Every program must be

approved through this office. There are so many needs that agencies seldom overlap. But we can't have all the medicines in one district and the house building in another. So we have our little tussles," he chuckled.

"Some groups are just getting started," he said "Russ O'Quinn's Foundation for Airborne Relief is planning air drops similar to what they did in Biafra. The Emergency Relief Fund had eighty-two people here for surveys. They've gone back to raise $600 million. Americans think big," he laughed.

"And are impatient. They arrive at the airport at 10:00 and want to have their pictures taken with the prime minister at 10:15. That is arranged if they offer a token gift to the prime minister's fund for the poor people who line up outside his house every day. We must set a minimum or Mujib would never get anything done. (The director of one agency told us the ante for seeing the Prime Minister was up to $7,000. "We couldn't afford that," he said.)

Which agency was doing the best job?

Choudhury rolled his eyes and waved his hands. "I don't like to pick, but since you asked me I must say CORR. They started during the cyclone and never stopped. They have the best organization and program, and the largest budget—$33 million. They work through their own bishops, priests, and churches. They already know the prime minister.

"Next to CORR, I would put the Protestant BERRS. They don't have a large local participation, but their funding program is brilliant. For one thing, they're buying boats which Bangladesh desperately needs.

"But don't take my word. Go see for yourselves."

We found the three-story CORR headquarters (an old mansion) at 23 Eskaton Road bustling with activity. "This work is so exciting I come to work early every morning," Nan

Borton, the perky public relations gal bubbled.

From Nan and two CORR leaders, Fathers Richard Timm and Charles Young, we learned the keys to CORR's success:

1. Multinational support from many Catholic and secular relief agencies. Europeans giving more than American Catholics. A contribution had even been received from the "Anti-Religious Citizen's Association" of Munich, Germany.

2. Streamlined coordinated organization reaching to village levels. Top people had to be Catholics; lower-echelon personnel could be of any faith.

3. Permanent rehabilitation instead of temporary relief. Goal of total rehabilitation of 200,000 familes (50,000 in each of the four dioceses). Food, clothing, medicines, seed, tools. Everything to make a family, even a bereft widow with children, self-sufficient.

4. Work instead of charity. One hundred thousand adults were currently employed on CORR projects.

CORR's files brimmed with interesting slices of success in the field.

Item: In the "widow village" of Modum Gram, where Pak soldiers shot eighteen men, CORR trained and equipped destitute women to make puffed rice candy for sale in Dacca markets.

Item: In Dinajpur CORR provided half the funds needed for vocational rehabilitation of lawyers, as requested by the local bar association. Italian Father Benjamin Labbe refused to buy barristers' wigs (a tradition learned from the British), on grounds the lawyers could grow their own hair.

Item: Also at Dinajpur a CORR "Power Tiller Center" was opened with 90 donated Japanese tillers, 18 Japanese instructors and 90 farmer trainees.

Item: Confronted with growing numbers of penniless women unable to feed their starving children, CORR Sisters at Barisal developed remunerative projects for penniless mothers. They gave the unskilled paste, empty milk powder bags, and waste paper and taught them to make paper bags for sale to shopkeepers. Women who could sew refashioned donated American and European clothing into Bengali saris and *lunghis* for distribution as relief goods. They were paid for their work with food.

Item: With $50,000 from the Norwegian Refugee Council and carpenter tools from Caritas, France, CORR put five thousand men to work in Dacca and Bakerganj.

BERRS was also housed in a converted residence near the ambitious but incomplete cluster of new government buildings. Like CORR, BERRS was also receiving more support from Europe than from the United States. Protestant groups in tiny Switzerland had given, by May 1, $598,966 while U.S. denominations had paid only $454,000. However, the books showed $1,973,000 as "pledges" and "potentials" from U.S. churches.

BERRS' medical director, Dr. Pueschel Johannes, a red-bearded German medical missionary borrowed from a Lutheran hospital in India, gave us some examples of how BERRS is spending its budgeted $12.4 million.

—Providing a million dollars to buy boats which the country desperately needs.

—Training and setting up widows and other war-affected women in a variety of occupations that include tailoring, sewing, weaving, secretarial, dyeing, and fish and fruit canning.

—Airlifting blankets, rice, powdered milk and other emergency supplies in a DC–4 and two DC–6 planes contracted from Norwegian companies. The DC–4, named *Moby Dick* was once President Eisenhower's personal plane.

—Purchasing a thousand hospital beds for government hospitals.

—Equipping an orthopedic hospital for the University of Dacca and footing sixty percent of the first year's budget.

"The greatest medical need," Dr. Johannes observed, "is to train more nationals in medicine and scatter them over the country. Ninety percent of the country's eight thousand doctors and 690 registered nurses live within a ten-mile radius of Dacca."

Rab Choudhury's list showed the Mennonite Central Committee third in agency participation. Bearded Maynard Shelley, MCC director for Bangladesh, quoted $300,000 for house building, food, and medicine during 1972, noting, "We hope to raise an additional three million."

Harry Martens, consultant for the Mennonite Foundation, compared his impressions of Bangladesh with Europe after World War II and the Palestinian refugees. "I've seen poverty just as bad," he said, "but never on such a massive scale as here."

We called on the Adventists. "Now we can share some of the grief of our Bengali friends," Jabil Jacobs said sadly. "We just buried our seventeen-year-old daughter. She was on an excursion and fell from a cliff. To think she was with us during much of the war and escaped harm."

Lois Jacobs served a delicious vegetarian meal. They talked about the future. "We've already started house building," Jabil said. "Our Seventh Day Adventist Welfare Service is hoping to raise $1 million for relief and rehabilitation here. We wish they could do more."

Troy Bennett said Southern Baptists expected to build a thousand houses and dig more tube wells.

World Vision was helping the hard-hit Garo tribal Baptists

in the north, rebuilding thirty Christian schools, resettling refugee families, providing plows, seed, and clothing. Roy Challberg, the field representative, called this "a drop in the bucket," adding, "There is need of every type in every direction you look."

Challberg remembered meeting a woman raped and pregnant by Pak soldiers. "She had considered taking her life but had five other children to support. Her desperation and fear were obvious. Through our interpreter, we told her we would pay for the expenses of having the baby and see that it was offered for adoption. She seemed happy and covered her face with her hands. We wept."

Everett Graffam (World Relief Commission) and George Hoffman (The Evangelical Alliance Relief Service of Britain) were conferring with evangelical missionaries. "We're giving through them," Graffam said. "They know where the need is and will be here to follow up." Graffam and Cal Olson had just presented $5,000 to the University of Dacca for work scholarships. "I wish we could do more. You know forty percent of the students are said to have been killed."

Graffam said his agency was supporting a feeding station manned by Howard Hawkes of the Assemblies of God at Khulna. "Three thousand women and children walk up to twenty-five miles for their cup of high-protein flour. Some arrive before daylight."

We set out to visit some of the countryside stations.

Enroute to Father Goedert's (by train, rickshaw, and on foot), we met Archbishop Ganguly on his motorcycle. "We almost despaired of life during the war," he recalled. "Now it's over and we're trying to rebuild. It will take a long time."

How was Father Goedert?

"Very weak physically, but strong spiritually. He still has his wit."

Our throats were cactus-dry when we reached Nagari about noon. Managing a smile on a lined face, the old warrior served us delicious homemade ice cream, then a meal.

While we ate, he reflected on the departure of the refugees. "When the war ended I told them to go home. They did. I think they were tired of eating wheat. I knew they preferred rice, but I didn't want them too happy or they'd stay indefinitely.

"We're still helping 131 villages with food and medicine. Seven or eight hundred are working for us in road repair. Carrying baskets of mud on their heads."

He grinned cannily. "I give them low pay. Our relief money goes further and they have incentive to find better jobs. You don't do the Bengalis any favor by making them dependent on you."

We caught up with Dr. Vic Olsen and his Bangladesh Brigade at the Abwey hospital south of Chittagong. "The Brigade is twenty-four students and a few others," he told us. "Sixteen of the students are from Wheaton College. They all came under Medical Assistance Programs in cooperation with our mission.

"The Brigade is financed with a $900,000 U.S. AID grant which MAP arranged. I took time off from furlough to be their leader. The kids are doing a tremendous job."

He presented the Brigade's two month program. "Our biggest thrust is to build houses and distribute household utensils for four thousand families before the monsoons start in June. We're also providing food and medicine and giving six hundred beds for government hospitals."

We asked Dr. Olsen about other relief work by the hospital and MAP. He quickly totaled some figures. "About two million dollars worth of drugs, plus about $600,000 in foodstuffs have come through MAP since the war ended. I say through

MAP because the drugs were donated by U.S. companies. The foodstuffs come through Food for the Hungry.

"Oh, I didn't mentioned the two Brigade nurses who are at the hospital to catch Benjabi babies. Benjabi," he explained,"is a name we made up for babies born of Punjabi fathers and Bengali mothers. The girls haven't 'caught' any yet, but Donn Ketcham keeps them busy with other cases."

"We wondered how the other Brigade members could possibly build four thousand houses in two months.

"By what we call positive reinforcement inducement," he said, "First the kids go into villages separately, with each one having an interpreter. In a village the Brigade member and his interpreter determine needs, order bamboo for the walls and sun grass for the roofs, and hire a local leader to encourage his people to build in a hurry. They accompany the materials back to the village, see that enough is loaded for part of the job. After a few days they go back and check progress, meet the payroll, and give the rest of the materials, At the final inspection they pay the local leader a bonus of two rupees (twenty-eight cents) for each house finished. Between times, they're working other villages on a coordinated basis. The entire house-building team keeps eighteen trucks, some from the U.N., going from daylight until dark. (Note: By June 12 the Brigade had built or repaired over ten thousand houses!)

We talked to the young people, saw their work. Dave Gottas, a pastor's son from Winnetka, Illinois, said, "Americans usually associate poverty with lack of money. But to know what it's really like, you've got to hear it, feel it, smell it."

Gary Sloan, a curly-haired sophomore from Indiana, expressed his feelings in a long prose poem as he imagined Christ was speaking to him. We quote in part,

. . . I have confronted you with an impossible task and problem
to solve, filled with countless widows, never-ending need, and
a pleading so often it soon becomes a duplicate of the one
before—
> You tried, did you then turn away frustrated,
>> turn away broken or hardened,
>> turn away?

I too saw the crowd, left the crowd, felt the crowd, and met
their inner loneliness.
I too felt their greedy tug, their impatient loudness, and their
shallow submission.
> and I too reacted
. . . . I too decided . . .
>> for I too was human.

Feel them, touch them my son—for as they touch you, they
touch me.
As you touch them—so too—it is I that you touch.
> I am hungry—
>> I am homeless—
>>> I am thirsty—
> I am a stranger—
>> I am naked—
>>> I am the one more.

Back in Dacca we eagerly devoured a newspaper to catch
up on world news. The most interesting item was the announcement of a son born in New Jersey to Paul and Ellen
Connett. They had named him Mujib after the Bangladesh
prime minister.

There was one more facet of the Bangladesh story we
wished to explore: the fate of the Bihari minority that had
sided with the Pak army.

We found hard information about the Biharis difficuilt to
come by. A hotel waiter told us that after finding a decapi-
tated man near a Bihari camp in Khulna, Bengalis had

stormed the camp, killing hundreds. Swedish missionary Goot Gustafson reported hearing gunfire every night around the Bihari camp near his house in Dacca.

We heard that about sixty-five thousand Biharis were in a camp just outside the capital's city limits. A reluctant taxi driver took us to the entrance. "The armed guards," our driver pointed out, "are not here to keep the Biharis in, but to keep their neighbors out."

The guards stood impassively as we walked into the camp. It appeared to be five square blocks in area. The mass of humanity that engulfed us suggested that the population estimate was not exaggerated. There were no tears in the haunting, hollowed eyes. They were beyond crying. They were not begging, but pleading, "Please tell the world about us. Please help us escape."

A Bihari doctor took us on a tour of despair. We saw dozens of shriveled gasping babies lying on the ground, fanned by emaciated mothers with shrunken breasts. "The mothers' breasts are dry," he said. "They have no milk nor are there fluids for the babies. That one will die tomorrow and the one over there might live three more days. They will all die soon." Then, voice rising higher, he wailed, "We are in a prison of fear. We cannot even go outside and bury our dead."

"Who is helping you?" we asked.

"The International Red Cross Committee *was* bringing a little food. Enough for a hundred calories per person each day. But they haven't come for the past two weeks."

"Why not?"

"We don't know," he answered despondently.

We put the plight of the Biharis before missionaries and Bengali leaders. "I know Christ forgave the thief on the cross," Anglican Matthew Malakar said. "I know I should forgive them. But knowing what they did to our people makes it very hard."

"I cannot condone what the Bengalis are doing to the Biharis," Phil Parshall said, "But having been here during the war, I can understand it. You must remember that in this culture it is an eye for an eye and a tooth for a tooth."

A veteran relief worker confided, "It's a very, very bad triangle. A million and a half Biharis are here. West Pakistan is holding four hundred thousand Bengalis caught there during the war. And India has ninety-one thousand Pakistan prisoners of war, some of which Sheik Mujib intends to put on trial for war crimes. The British have been trying to mediate, but I guess tensions are still too high."

"But what about the Biharis *now*?"

He shrugged. "They are dying every day. We can do nothing. It's politically impossible for a foreign relief agency to help them. The government says, 'Help our Bengalis first.' "

Nevertheless, the Mennonites were giving food and medicine in one camp at Khulna. "How long we can continue, we don't know," Maynard Shelley said.

Shelley is a deep, thoughtful, sensitive man, a portrait in sad-eyed humility. "I have no faith in religion or religious systems, especially when those religious systems have access to armies and bombs," he said bluntly. "I do have faith in Jesus Christ. I don't want a religion that hides Him. I want a community of disciples to reveal Him and proclaim Him because they are concerned about the people for whom Christ was concerned—the poor, the children, the women, the oppressed, the outcasts."

It seemed to us the Mennonite was expressing the heartbeat of true Christianity which Jesus described a few days before His death.

"I was hungry and you gave me food. I was thirsty and you gave me drink. I was lonely and you made me welcome. I was naked and you clothed me. I was ill and you came and looked after me. I was in prison and you came to see me there."

Then the true men will answer him: 'Lord, when did we see you hungry and give you food? When did we see you thirsty and give you something to drink? When did we see you lonely and make you welcome, or see you naked and clothe you, or see you ill or in prison and go to see you?"

And the king will reply, "I assure you that whatever you did for the humblest of my brothers you did for me" (Matthew 25:35-40, Phillips).

For Those Who Wish to Help

BANGLADESH is out of the headlines, but relief and rehabilitation continue. For readers wishing to contribute, the authors suggest that gifts be marked "Bangladesh Aid" and sent through one of the following channels:

Your church or denominational headquarters.

Assembly of God Foreign Mission Department, 1445 Boonville Ave., Springfield, Mo. 65802.

Association of Baptists for World Evangelism, 1620 Springdale Rd., Cherry Hill, N.J. 08034.

Baptist World Alliance, 1628 16th St. N.W., Washington D.C. 20009.

CARE, 660 First Ave., New York, N.Y. 10016.

Catholic Medical Mission Board, 10 West 17th St., New York, N.Y. 10011.

Catholic Relief Services, 350 Fifth Ave., New York,N.Y., 10001 (CARITAS for Catholics outside the U.S.).

Christian Organization for Relief and Rehabilitation (CORR), 23 New Eskaton Rd., Dacca 2, Bangladesh.

Churches of God in North America, 421 Villa Rose Dr., Springfield, Mo, 65802.

Church World Service, 475 Riverside Dr., New York, N.Y. 10027.

Food for the Hungry, 1115 Colorado Blvd., Los Angeles, Calif. 90041.

Foundation for Airborne Relief, 2680 Wardlow Rd. E., Long Beach, Calif. 90807.

Holt Adoption Program, P.O. Box 95, Creswell, Ore. 97426.

Lutheran World Relief, Inc., 315 Park Ave. S., New York, N.Y. 10010.

International Christian Fellowship, 107 N. Hale St., Wheaton, Ill. 60187.

Medical Assistance Programs, P.O. Box 50, Wheaton, Ill. 60187.

Mennonite Central Committee, Akron, Pa. 17501

OXFAM, 274 Banbury Rd., Oxford, England.

Partnership Mission, P.O. Box 805, Wheaton, Ill. 60187 (provides gift Bibles).

Seventh Day Adventist Relief Services, 6840 Eastern Ave., N.W., Washington, D.C. 20012.

Southern Baptist Convention, Foreign Mission Board, P.O. Box 6597, Richmond, Va. 23230

The Evangelical Relief Fund, 19 Draycott Pl., London, S.W. 3, England.

World Relief Commission of the National Association Of Evangelicals, P.O. Box 44, Valley Forge, Pa. 19481.

World Vision International, Box 0, Pasadena, Calif. 91100.

Appreciations

BANGLADESH was to us only a distant boil on the backside of the world when Ray Knighton, president of Medical Assistance Programs, called. "You *must* meet Dr. Viggo Olsen, a medical missionary just back from Bangladesh," he insisted. "He's in my office right now."

Our free-lance schedule was packed, but Ray Knighton's "must" could not be ignored.

Meeting Dr. Olsen was only the teaser. The more we dug, the more certain we felt that here was the great, untold story of the ugly, just-concluded war.

Harper & Row thought so, too, and within the month we were winging thirty hours to the shattered little country that has so grabbed the heartstrings of the world.

We never met a friendlier people than the Bengalis (so long as they knew we did not represent the U.S. government), nor missionaries more deserving of having their stories told. Many books could be written about the heroic service of individual missionaries (two will be forthcoming by other authors). Yet we felt this book had to highlight what all missionaries and church-related relief groups had done amidst the crimson backdrop of unprecedented atrocities and human suffering.

To this end, the Protestant and Catholic groups represented were enthusiastically cooperative. They opened their files and their missionary representatives in Bangladesh opened their hearts. Bengali churchmen and government officials were equally cooperative and helpful.

To all we are grateful, but we express special thanks to a few:

Rab Choudhury, Bangladesh Coordinator for External Relief and Rehabilitation, for the Bengali point of view on Christian relief work.

Matthew Malakar, secretary-treasurer of the Bangladesh Christian Council, for perspective on Christianity in his new country.

Dr. Viggo Olsen, of the Association of Baptists for World Evangelism, for orientation and aid in obtaining visas. (Dr. Olsen holds U.S. Visa No. 1 from the Bangladesh government —this in honor of his service.) His autobiography, *Daktar-Diplomat of Bangladesh*, with Jeannette Lockerbie, will be published by Moody Press this year.

The Reverend Rochunga Pudaite and Mr. Daineikung Pudaite of Partnership Mission for special assistance in their native India.

The Reverend Troy Bennett, a missionary for the Southern Baptist Convention, for assistance with Dacca contacts.

Mrs. Nan Barton, public relations officer of the Catholic-related Christian Organization for Relief and Rehabilitation (CORR), for introductions to Catholic relief workers and missionaries.

For editorial direction we are indebted to Clayton Carlson,

editor-manager of Harper & Row's Religious Books Department. His enthusiasm was contagious; his guidance kept us on the right track.

For manuscript preparation we are obliged to our loyal secretary, Mrs. Paula Kelly.

73 74 75 10 9 8 7 6 5 4 3 2 1